CRACK THE CODE OF BECOMING A LIFETIME MILLIONAIRE

The roadmap of creating a lifetime of wealth, Achieving financial freedom, Generational wealth building And Wealth creation rules.

By

RICHARD J. BICKFORD

Crack the code of Becoming a lifetime millionaire

Copyright

All rights reserved. No parts of this publication may be reproduced, distributed, or transmitted in any form or any means, including photocopying, recording, or other electronic or mechanical methods, without the prior written permission of the publisher, except in the case of brief quotations embodied in critical reviews and certain other non-commercial uses permitted by copyright law.

Copyright © (Richard J. Bickford),
(2024)

Crack the code of Becoming a lifetime millionaire

TABLE OF CONTENT

INTRODUCTION 4
   Unveiling the mysteries of wealth 4
   THE PSYCHOLOGY OF WEALTH 7
CHAPTER 2 13
   FINANCIAL MINDSET MASTERY 13
   MOVING FROM SCARCITY TO ABUNDANCE 18
   CULTIVATING A WEALTH CONSCIOUSNESS 23
CHAPTER 3 37
   SETTING "SMART" FINANCIAL GOALS 37
CHAPTER 4 42
   BUDGETING FOR SUCCESS 42
   SAVING AND INVESTING STRATEGIES 49
CHAPTER 5 57
   ENTREPRENEURSHIP AND WEALTH CREATION 57
   NAVIGATING THE ENTREPRENEUR'S JOURNEY 62
   IDENTIFYING BUSINESS OPPORTUNITIES 66
CHAPTER 6 78
   Investing wisely 78
   UNDERSTANDING DIFFERENT INVESTMENT VEHICLES 78
   RISK MANAGEMENT FOR INVESTMENT 90
CHAPTER 7 98
   LEVERAGING REAL ESTATE FOR WEALTH 98
   SMART PROPERTY INVESTMENT STRATEGIES 104
CHAPTER 8 106
   Living Rich For A Lifetime 106
   LIFESTYLE DESIGN FOR WEALTH 106
   CREATING A BALANCED AND FULFILLING LIFE 112
   THE ROLE OF HEALTH AND WELLNESS IN WEALTH 118
CHAPTER 9 122
   PASSING DOWN WEALTH TO FUTURE GENERATIONS 122
   ESTATE PLANNING AND LEGACY BUILDING 131

CHAPTER 10 .... **134**
   Mastering the Art of Giving Back.. 134
   PHILANTHROPY AND SOCIAL IMPACT.. 134
   BUILDING A WEALTHY COMMUNITY.. 139
CHAPTER 11..**150**
   CONCLUSION... 150

INTRODUCTION

Unveiling the mysteries of wealth

Many of us only give money a second thought when our circumstances force us to.
The agony of losing everything also compels us to take action. What I discovered at a very young age enabled me to rise above my horrible circumstances. I started producing money because of my parents' advice to never chase money and instead concentrate on finding solutions for other people's issues.

In fast forward to thirty years later, I quit my nine to five senior information technology job and began my entrepreneurial journey after overcoming obstacle after obstacle, winning battle after battle, and devoting a significant amount of time, money, and energy to cross-disciplinary study, research, and ample experience as a coach assisting others in generating more than a billion pounds.

My client Sarah, a young professional, recognized the value of early financial education and signed up for my Wealth Breakthrough Coaching Program at COVID-19. She committed herself to comprehending how her financial actions were influenced by her subconscious and her beliefs. We focused on her debt management, money-making and saving methods, and investing ideas. Equipped with expertise, she made prudent financial decisions, enabling her to establish a stable financial base.

Crack the code of Becoming a lifetime millionaire

In summary, knowing why some people become wealthy while others do not can enable people to take control of their financial futures. By adopting the proper mindset, pursuing financial education, establishing objectives, cultivating resilience, grasping chances, forming networks, never stopping learning, and obtaining coaching from experts, anyone can start along the path to financial riches.

Are you sick and weary of just scraping by from paycheck to paycheck? Have you ever wondered why some people manage to amass fortune with such ease, while others find it difficult to make ends meet? The fact is that building wealth involves much more than just saving money and working hard. Contrary to popular belief, the psychology of wealth actually has a considerably greater impact.

In the process of making money and succeeding, a few psychological aspects must be considered. Mentality is one of the most significant considerations. Your potential to create riches can be significantly impacted by your mindset towards money and wealth. You will always find it difficult to accumulate wealth if you think of money as being scarce and difficult to get by. You will, however, be far more likely to draw wealth into your life if you adopt an abundant mindset and think that there is always enough money for everyone.

Your views on money and achievement are a significant psychological component as well. Many people are prevented from reaching their full potential by restricting ideas. You might think, for instance, that you're not bright, intelligent, or fortunate enough to become wealthy. These restrictive ideas have the potential to be very potent and can keep you from taking the required actions to build the life you've always wanted.

When it comes to creating riches, motivation is another important component. Building wealth requires a great deal of effort and commitment, and it's simple to lose motivation along the route. Having a strong feeling of motivation and purpose is crucial for this reason. It's lot simpler to keep motivated and focused when you know what you're working toward.

What then can you do to break through limiting ideas, cultivate a wealth mindset, and maintain motivation while pursuing success? Learning about the psychology of wealth is one of the best things you can do. Study the routines and attitudes of prosperous individuals, then make an effort to incorporate those similar routines and attitudes into your own life. Seek for mentors who can offer you guidance on your journey and surround yourself with positive influences.

The psychology of wealth ultimately boils down to knowing yourself and your own perspectives on success and money. You can begin to draw prosperity and success into your life by being conscious of your own psychological inclinations and making an effort to change them for the better. Thus, dedicate some time to exploring the intriguing field of wealth psychology and begin building the life of your desires right now!

THE PSYCHOLOGY OF WEALTH

Everyone aspires to be affluent. How can one get wealthy? Get rich quick schemes abound in our marketplaces, but it's crucial to realize that being wealthy is largely psychological in nature—you're trapped in the top-to-bottom cash flow. Does someone need to know finance? Indeed, it is! because the debt from your grandfather's funeral and your children's bills will never be paid off. Your dream automobiles won't buy themselves, and neither will your house build itself. Thus, acquiring wealth requires a thorough understanding of finance, which also requires a thorough comprehension of the fundamental psychology involved in accumulating wealth and becoming wealthy.

Let's begin with the initial query. What distinguishes being wealthy from being rich? A few weeks ago, I recall posing this query to a buddy. He clarified, saying that being wealthy entailed having a large amount of cash on hand. Money to spend on whatever you want, whenever you want. Conversely, amassing a large number of assets was a sign of affluence. I wholeheartedly concurred with her definition, but what then turns into a benefit? The vehicle? The terrain? The home? An asset is any piece of property that belongs to a person or business, is valued, and can be used to pay off debts, obligations, or bequeaths. Have you ever heard of someone being called a "asset," even when their career is just getting started? This brings us to the obvious distinction between being wealthy and rich: the former worry about money constantly, while the latter don't.

We probably belong in the first group. We may be wealthy in the sense that we make higher-than-average salaries, but we struggle to build up any true wealth due to our spending (properties, vehicles, lifestyles, etc.) and occasionally bad choices. Our starting this financial adventure very late in life is another handicap; in school, we are not exposed to any meaningful entrepreneurial classes or income-generating companies. After graduating from school, we have numerous pathophysiological cascades in our brains, which ultimately cause poverty. We become entangled in the never-ending rat race, usually living hand to mouth as we mature. Get hitched, have children, and labor till our death. Now is the moment to liberate yourself and delve into the psychology of money.

Financial freedom ultimately has more to do with wealth. It indicates that you do not exist paycheck to paycheck. It indicates that you have either amassed enough savings to support your lifestyle without requiring you to work every day or that you have sufficient passive income streams to be earning money while you sleep.

I don't really need the nice house or the automobiles, so I don't really care about being perceived as wealthy. All I want is to be able to take time off from work whenever I want to, without worrying about money, so that I can spend more time with my family. The saying "wealth is measured in time, not dollars" is something I seem to have read somewhere, and I firmly think it to be accurate.

I'll give a definition now. an archetype. Universal, innate models of persons, actions, or personalities known as archetypes have an impact on human behavior. They stand for common themes and imagery from the collective unconscious. Similar to how we inherit innate behavioral tendencies, we inherit these archetypes as well. Such an archetype is wealth. We can learn more about the nature of riches and, most importantly, start to comprehend what it means to each of us personally by looking at the universal archetype of wealth. It's surprising how much scarcity thinking creeps in when you don't have much money. The negative scarcity perspective holds that there is never enough of something to go around. When you catch yourself thinking that way, make every effort to shift your perspective to one of abundance.

First and foremost, one must acknowledge that money does not grow on trees and that nothing falls from the sky. Acquiring money requires a lot of optimism, believing that you have already earned it as well as the discipline needed to maintain and grow it. If you Google "how to earn passive income," you'll find a ton of websites with sequential lists of things to buy. You are ignorant of the fact that the website manager, who has dedicated time and expertise to learning how to build and administer a website, makes additional money just by clicking any of the hyperlinks. Investing in oneself is the finest possible investment you can make. Like learning to play an instrument, developing your talents, skills, creative ideas, goals, and vision requires regular practice and honing. But remember that knowledge is power and that this is a process! It never hurts to set aside a few minutes each day for reading. It actually sharpens your thinking and enhances your memory. This is the initial route for generating riches and ascending the wealth hierarchy.

I still recall finishing up school and doing that initial Google search. "How can I make money?" I had no hope! I had very high expectations and was always thinking about how to reach them, day and night. I had many sleepless nights as a result of this, but I thought the late nights and early mornings would eventually pay off. The will to succeed is considerably more crucial than knowledge or prophecies. It holds greater significance than the past, education, finances, situations, achievements and setbacks, or the opinions, words, or deeds of others. It is more significant than talent, abilities, or looks. It may make or shatter an organization, a home, a friendship, and a business.

Attempting a no-risk matched betting is typically the first choice to appear on the Google search result page; this method is arguably the simplest. It is a method of betting that people utilize to benefit from bookmakers' free bets and other promotions. Because it is based on applying a mathematical equation rather than chance, it is typically regarded as risk-free. It can take some time to understand how to wager on matches, which is presumably why fewer people participate in it. Some individuals just perceive it as gambling and find it hard to believe there are no risks involved. Okay, so it's not for everyone. It is gambling, in my opinion. I promise you that when you are linked to the proper source, this existence isn't a gamble, despite what some individuals may unintentionally say!

Regretfully, excessive gambling can have a negative impact on your personal finances since it can get overwhelming to try to recover losses. In addition to spending earnings, savings, and extra money, debts resulting from loans and borrowings to offset gambling losses can also be a characteristic of problem gambling. Losing money isn't the only effect of compulsive gambling, though. Problem gamblers frequently claim that their lonesome attempts to chase losses make them feel alone. There is a propensity to avoid employment, education, and college in order to gamble. A fixation with gambling, a lack of interest in preserving relationships, and a lack of drive to participate in social activities are also common.

A few more strategies are working a part-time job, launching a side business, and building a website. These tasks typically take a great deal of dedication and optimism to continue, especially in the face of difficulty. However, remember that persistence and determination are necessary for success, and that perseverance and energy overcome any obstacles.

It all comes down to being resourceful; some of these extra income-generating techniques depend on certain locations, while others don't. Everybody has been in a difficult situation at some point in their life, but everything is possible for someone who is committed.

Contrary to what some would have you believe, there is no one correct way to get wealthy. whether or not through formal schooling. It is difficult for anyone hoping to make flawless predictions about the next twenty to thirty years because of these times of uncertainty. I've discovered that while there are factors outside of our control, you still need to keep the optimistic mindset associated with riches.

It is in our instinct as humans to evaluate ourselves against others. Regretfully, we live in a world that excels at measuring and comparing externals because we can only compare what we can objectively measure. Somewhere along the line, we came to believe that comparing people's homes, vehicles, incomes, and wardrobes would allow us to identify who is leading a better life. To put it plainly, we linked net value to self-worth. As a sad consequence, we started valuing our own lives based solely on the things we owned. However, the things we own are not nearly as valuable as our lives. "Our lives are made possible by our wages, but they do not define who we are."

The core of self-worth and self-respect is this. Financial success is often linked to feelings of stability, worthiness, and belonging, yet money doesn't usually address personal issues; rather, money solves financial issues. Without an unbroken core of self, it will be hard to achieve financial wealth or any other kind of true success. Possession of money does not always translate into respect or self-worth. Conversely, it appears that obtaining a life of genuine wealth and prosperity requires having high self-esteem and respect for oneself.

CHAPTER 2

FINANCIAL MINDSET MASTERY

When it comes to accomplishing personal and business goals, money is often seen as a key indicator of success. The money mindset is simply your attitude toward money, thus cultivating a positive attitude about money is critical for overall success and well-being.

To develop a positive money attitude, first clear your mind of any limiting ideas that are blocking you from taking action, and then begin viewing the world through an opportunistic lens in order to fully accomplish wealth in your life.

If you want to develop a good money mindset, here are some tangible measures to take.

What is a Positive Money Mindset?
If changing your money attitude is a top goal, you should first understand what a money mindset actually is. A money mindset is a general attitude toward your finances.

Your daily financial decisions are influenced by your money thinking. This can have a significant impact on your capacity to meet your objectives. It is critical for success to cultivate a positive financial mindset.

While money can be a frustrating topic for many people, changing your perspective on money allows you to make better decisions about how to overcome obstacles.

The Four Steps to Create a Positive Money Mindset

Money and mindset are inextricably linked, so understanding them and focusing on how to see them positively is critical for long-term success. But here's a secret: as you improve your relationship with money, you'll see a significant improvement in many other areas of your life.

Here are four methods to help you build a positive financial mindset:

- Forgive Your Financial Mistakes.

If you've never missed a credit card payment or bill, you might as well be a financial expert. However, for the vast majority, it is critical to forgive your financial missteps.
The idea is to redirect your attention away from shame and make room for new habits and a more positive attitude about money in the future.

To forgive your financial mistakes, first admit what happened, apologize to yourself, and then concentrate on going forward. If you begin to develop a negative attitude about money, remember that your financial blunders do not define you. You are not defined by your previous financial blunders.

- Set financial goals.

Setting financial objectives once you've forgiven past financial blunders might be an excellent next step in mastering your money mindset. When making goals, identify what is most important to you and include everything on the table.
You'll want to look at what goals are within reach, which will take some time, and which will need to be part of your long-term plan.

Once you've identified your financial goals, use the SMART goal technique to ensure they're Specific, Measurable, Achievable, Relevant, and Timely.

- Optimize Your Budget for Happiness.

It is not easy to grasp the money mindset. However, adjusting your budget to incorporate items that make you happy will make things a bit easier. If a gym membership or going out to dinner makes you happy, make sure you budget for these expenses. If you don't feel deprived, budgeting will be less of a bother.

When budgeting, a decent rule of thumb is to allocate 50% of your wages to needs such as housing, food, petrol, and prescriptions, 30% to wants such as vacations and learning to play an instrument, and 20% to savings. If you have debt, the 20% may be used to pay it off first.

- Inform yourself about money.

Finally, if you want to maintain a favorable attitude toward money, educate yourself about it. Surround yourself with others who share those values, read books that promote positive mindsets, and make sure your social media feeds do not promote negative attitudes toward money and spending.

Read Books.
Your money-related feelings have a direct impact on your financial situation. While your parents and other external forces have instilled diverse financial

The good news is that your money-related thoughts can alter.

The goal is to keep feeding your mind with new and positive stuff that will educate you how to think about money in a completely new way.

Money mentality books promote positive money spending habits and budgeting, which are essential for your money mindset training.

Get Inspiration from Quotes
Surrounding yourself with motivational and useful quotes will help you develop the right money mentality. Look for statements that make you feel good about yourself and your spending habits, then save them to your phone or computer or print them to keep about the house.

Follow Successful People.
Stay up to date with successful individuals. Following successful people, whether through social media, a blog, or reliable news channels, will motivate you to achieve greatness.

These folks do not have to be public figures. Challenge yourself to only seek advise from those who have already accomplished what you aspire to achieve.
These individuals may be family members, coworkers, mentors, or financial influences. Whatever the situation, it's far easier to follow in the footsteps of someone who has previously achieved success and has a positive money mindset.

Set goals for a financially successful future.
Now that you've learned how to cultivate a good "money mindset," put these recommendations into action for a more prosperous future. Setting objectives now can prepare you for financial success in the future.

MOVING FROM SCARCITY TO ABUNDANCE

What is the scarcity mindset?
Scarcity mindset refers to a continuous sense of not having enough—whether it's time, money, or connection. A scarcity mindset can be a self-fulfilling prophecy, as these ideas make it difficult to go forward and may keep you stuck in shortage.
Scarcity is more than a mindset for many people. If you are having difficulty meeting your fundamental necessities such as affording food, housing, and paying your bills, it is not your fault and cannot be solved with a simple mental adjustment.

Growing up in poverty, or in actual scarcity, has been related to behavioral and mental health issues[2], as it literally affects your brain.

Adopting an abundant mindset will not immediately fix all of your problems, but it may help you see things in a different light, making it simpler to solve or cope.

Signs of Scarcity Mindset
It is crucial to highlight that some of the symptoms and feelings associated with a scarcity mindset may be comparable to sadness or other mental health issues, and scarcity can also cause mental health problems.

Here are some symptoms you could have a scarcity mindset:
- Feeling overwhelmed with bills and duties.
- Overschedule yourself
- Accepting opportunities that aren't suited for you because you're frightened another one won't arrive

If your scarcity mindset is interfering with your daily functioning, you should consult a mental health expert.

How A Scarcity Mindset Can Affect You

If you've ever made a hurried decision because you didn't have time to consider the ramifications, you understand what it's like to make decisions with a scarcity mindset since time is limited for you.
This is because our minds have limited bandwidth at any given time. Constantly thinking ahead about how to outsmart consumes bandwidth, resulting in lower cognitive ability which can lead to self-defeating acts.

Operating at this level of diminished brainpower can result in activities that are ultimately self-defeating but feel (or may be) out of your control. Some include:

- Engaging less regularly with preventative healthcare.
- Not sticking to recommended meds
- Being less inclined to follow up on appointments in general.
- Symptoms may include decreased productivity at work or home, as well as an inability to provide attentive parenting.
- Making inappropriate financial decisions

In this exhausted state, your brain activity slows in the prefrontal cortex[4] (the area of the brain concerned with decision making), similar to a computer attempting to do too many functions at once. Decision-making

response times are longer, resulting in increased stress and decreased confidence. Long-term planning becomes very burdensome.
Scarcity on a bigger scale can also have an impact on people's mindsets and decisions. It is considered that events such as the 2008 financial crisis (and, more likely, the coronavirus epidemic and the
resulting economic instability) have harmed the ability to make swift decisions.

Cultivating an abundance mindset.
This means that adopting the contrary, an abundance or growth mindset, results in benefits such as improved performance and greater brain malleability. Our brains receive a dopamine boost when we take risks and successfully finish them, preparing us to seek more dopamine by increasing the growth behaviors that caused the dopamine release in the first place.

- Acceptance

You may wish to improve your situation in life—this is part of the development mindset!—but accepting it helps you move forward. By doing so, you cease wasting your limited resources fighting against accepting your current situation. To know where you're heading, you must first know where you started.

- Self-Compassion

Whatever you've done in your life has led you to where you are today, and you should be proud of yourself for getting there. Any habit or mindset you desire to modify had a cause or purpose at one time: survival. Give yourself some self-compassion.

- Find That One Thing.

Perhaps your money are limited, but you have plenty of free time. Consider this an area of abundance in your life to be appreciated. Or you have a lot of money but not enough time since you work so hard to earn it. You might admit that you wish you could spend more time with your family, but your abundance benefits them.

Don't have a lot of time or money? Perhaps you have a lot of love from a person or a pet. No matter how minor, there is probably at least one thing in your life that you consider abundant rven if it's simply the fact that you breathed again today.

- Define Abundance for yourself.

Everyone's perception of abundance and an affluent mindset varies. What appears to be abundance to one person may appear to be scarcity to another, and vice versa. It's difficult to get into the attitude of abundance if you don't know what you're striving for. How does it feel to be abundant? What would your life be like?

- Start small.

Changing all of your habits or ways of thinking at once in any domain can result in unrealistic expectations. What areas do you believe your scarcity attitude is most limiting?

Begin by making modest changes to your mentality there. Do you feel like your time is limited these days? Consider what you enjoy doing with your time and what you might be able to provide.

Mindfulness

Our brains understandably get caught up in the scarcity concept. They are always considering what they should do next to survive. This takes us out of the present. Taking some time to be mindful, whether through meditation or simply paying attention to the present moment—can help our brains slow down and allow us to think more clearly.

Journaling can aid in defining personal abundance by identifying areas of abundance and places for improvement.

CULTIVATING A WEALTH CONSCIOUSNESS

Wealth consciousness, money consciousness, money Mindset , attracting wealth.
After chatting with a client, I reflected about wealth consciousness. I was astonished by my client's belief system around money.
Ideas of shortage and limitation in any notion in life repel any degree of plenty from us. The world is filled with wealth. It's all around us, yet we choose to focus on the fact that "there's not enough".
If money does not come readily to you or does not appear to stick to you, you may need to reconsider your assumptions about wealth.

What do you believe about money?
 You are not alone in believing that having money makes you selfish or bad. Some people believe that a lack of money is a spiritual issue, with phrases like "God wants me to struggle" or "God must not want me to have money."

If this sounds like you, your financial perspective needs to alter. To attract and create more money for yourself and your family, you must first unlearn concepts of scarcity or limitation, and then learn to live a life of persistent wealth consciousness.

Wealth Consciousness: I am not worthy.

People's definitions of success vary. However, having riches in our lives allows us to better care for the people we care about the most, including ourselves.

To grow your money consciousness, you must think that you can achieve prosperity in your life. Anything is possible for you; you must believe it! When it comes to acquiring money, we must be able to imagine ourselves becoming increasingly wealthy. It doesn't matter how brilliant or talented we are, or if we're sitting on the finest business opportunity of our lives. We will struggle to develop money if we do not believe we can do so because of who we are or where we are in life.

Wealth flows to people who think they deserve it. It flows to people who picture it in their hands, bank accounts, and lifestyles.

"Rich people have small TVs and big libraries, and poor people have small libraries and big TVs." ~Zig Ziglar

Wealth Consciousness: Mindset and Identity

I recall being told that you needed to get an education, master a skill, and work hard for money. Even as a child, I had developed a bad attachment with money.

To put it mildly, my belief system was limited. As a young adult, and for many years afterward, my thinking was closed to the notion that my ability to accumulate riches was endless. I believed it was impossible to create wealth of any type with the cards I was dealt. Wealth consciousness, wealth attitude, attract wealth

Knowing that our attitudes toward money can be influenced from an early age, how do you believe yours was? Have you always assumed that money would be difficult to obtain?

Limiting ideas are amplified when they become part of our identity. Do you identify more with a poor or middle-class family? Many of us can't envision what it would be like to travel to exotic destinations and spend time with wealthy people because it's "just not who we are."

What is your attitude toward others who are wealthy? It is a frequent fallacy that affluent people are arrogant, harsh, and judgmental of the poor. It's unsurprising that believing such things about rich individuals could prevent you from actively chasing wealth - even if only subconsciously.

Wealth Consciousness: Do you want to be wealthy?
You now understand what is partially preventing you from accumulating wealth. Next, ask yourself if you are ready to shift your money mindset.

Do you feel ready to examine your mentality and the constraints you've placed on yourself? When we look in the mirror and see our own flaws or limitations, we may be dissatisfied. Rather than using your anger to criticize or condemn yourself, channel it into something beneficial.

Having a positive perspective about money creation can keep you doing what feels right, even when life throws you curveballs and your world gets chaotic. Even if no one else believes in your objectives and desires, you can still take inspired action.

The only way to get all of the money and prosperity you deserve is to have a clear wealth consciousness and to keep going forward.

Understand that none of this will happen unless you start with a clear vision. You must envision yourself with the prosperity and abundance you desire and deserve. Every day, locate a quiet area and see yourself having the financial freedom, flexibility, and life you want!

Creating a Vision of Wealth
Creating money is a journey that takes commitment, strategy, and a clear sense of purpose. The value of vision in wealth development cannot be emphasized. A clear and compelling vision can help individuals navigate the route to financial success.

Individuals who have a vision for success are more likely to make sound judgments and take the required efforts to make their dreams a reality. A strong vision can bring drive, focus, and clarity, allowing people to stay on track and overcome any challenges that arise.

Throughout this chapter, we will investigate the function of vision in wealth development and provide insights into how individuals might harness this tremendous force to build long-term prosperity.
Vision is important in wealth development because it sets the framework for your goals and aspirations. It enables you to focus on what is genuinely important and devise a practical plan of action to achieve your goals.

Having a vision allows you to create a success-oriented mindset and take the required efforts to attain your financial goals. Whether you want to save for retirement, invest in real estate, or start a new business, your vision can lead you to the appropriate decisions and actions.

Furthermore, creating wealth is a long-term endeavor that takes patience, discipline, and dedication. With a clear financial vision, you may stay motivated and devoted to your objectives even when faced with difficulties or unforeseen barriers.

Furthermore, understanding the ideas of wealth development and having a good financial vision can allow you to make informed decisions and capitalize on market possibilities. Whether you're looking to invest in a promising business or buy a rental property, having a clear vision and plan of action may help you make the correct decisions and accumulate money over time.

The Power of Vision in Creating Wealth
Building wealth and long-term financial success necessitates a clear sense of purpose. Vision is vital in this situation. Having a clear vision can help people take the required measures to grow money, make informed decisions, and eventually realize their financial goals.

When creating a vision for wealth creation, it is critical to devise a detailed and realistic plan. This enables the identification of opportunities and future obstacles, which can be addressed proactively. Individuals with a strong vision might develop a purpose-driven plan to achieve their financial goals.

Vision also provides drive and focus during the wealth generating process. It ignites creativity and motivates people to pursue their goals, especially when faced with hurdles or disappointments.

Finally, achieving money through a vision necessitates perseverance and dedication to a long-term strategy. Individuals can achieve long-term prosperity and financial success by connecting their activities with the vision.

Strategic Planning for Wealth Creation
Effective strategic planning is critical in the pursuit of wealth growth. Without a clear vision, it might be difficult to make informed judgments and take the required steps to build wealth.

A vision-driven strategy can provide clarity and direction during the planning process, ensuring that each decision aligns with the ultimate goal of creating wealth.

Whether creating short-term or long-term goals, a vision-driven attitude will help you uncover opportunities and avoid potential traps along the road. Individuals who focus on strategic wealth planning might improve their chances of success and achieve their financial goals faster. Anyone may strive toward wealth creation and financial freedom by harnessing the power of vision and using a strategic planning approach.

Developing a Visionary Mindset

Creating wealth through vision necessitates a specific attitude that fosters and encourages a visionary approach to wealth creation. The ability to match one's thoughts, attitudes, and actions with a clear vision is critical for producing long-term wealth. It is critical to stay focused on the broad picture and avoid becoming weighed down by short-term obstacles or setbacks along the way.

The key to having a visionary mentality is to stay committed to the idea while remaining adaptable and evolving to new conditions. This entails having the guts to take measured risks and make difficult decisions that are consistent with the larger picture.

Individuals who stay focused on the long term and cultivate a growth-oriented attitude can produce wealth through vision in a sustainable and self-fulfilling manner. It is critical to keep the vision at the forefront of the wealth creation journey and to periodically monitor progress to ensure alignment with the ultimate aim of wealth accumulation.

The Visionary Mindset: A Checklist

Stay committed to the vision, especially when faced with adversity.
Be open to new opportunities and perspectives.
Take reasonable risks in line with long-term aims.
Stay flexible and adaptable to changing conditions.
Regularly evaluate progress and alter the course as necessary.
A visionary mindset is the foundation of vision-driven wealth creation, providing the inspiration and tenacity required to build long-term wealth and achieve financial success.

Overcoming Challenges and Obstacles

When it comes to producing money, individuals frequently face a variety of hurdles and impediments that can prevent them from attaining their financial objectives. These challenges can take numerous forms, ranging from growing costs and economic insecurity to personal setbacks and unforeseen life occurrences. Those who can sustain a solid vision throughout the journey, on the other hand, will find incentive to keep going, even in the face of adversity.

It's important to remember that a strong vision is more than just a tool for planning and strategizing during prosperous times. Rather, it is an important part of developing resilience and perspective when dealing with adversity and unexpected failures. Individuals who have a clear vision of the final objective are better equipped to deal with unforeseen problems and setbacks while remaining focused on their financial goals.

Staying in the Course

One of the most difficult components of wealth accumulation can be sticking the course in the face of setbacks. It is easy to become disheartened or overwhelmed when the path appears arduous, and losing sight of the end goal can have long-term consequences on the path to financial success. Those who keep a clear vision, on the other hand, can better regulate their emotions and stay focused on the task at hand, allowing them to continue working toward their goals.

Furthermore, difficulties and challenges can frequently present unique possibilities for growth and learning. Individuals who maintain a flexible vision can alter their goals and methods in reaction to new information or changing circumstances, resulting in greater resilience and preparedness to face whatever comes their way.

Summary: Overcoming barriers and problems is a necessary component of the wealth generation process. Individuals can, however, discover the perseverance and drive necessary to press forward in the face of hardship by retaining a solid vision and being focused on the ultimate goal. Furthermore, by perceiving setbacks as chances for growth and learning, people can cultivate a flexible and adaptable mindset that will help them on their journey to financial success.

Adapting and Evolving With Vision
As individuals move on their path to vision-driven wealth creation, it is critical to stay adaptable and open to change. Adapting one's vision can result in continuing growth and financial success. It is critical to assess the feasibility and relevance of the original vision, ensuring that it is consistent with current circumstances and aims. Individuals can take advantage of fresh possibilities and overcome any hurdles that may arise in their pursuit of achievement.

Maintaining a growth mentality is essential for adjusting and evolving with vision. Individuals who embrace obstacles and seek out opportunities for learning and development can broaden their vision and propel themselves to even greater heights of accomplishment.

Finally, staying true to the original idea while adapting it to current reality can lead to long-term success in wealth development. Individuals who link their behaviors with the vision can stay focused on attaining their long-term financial goals and living a joyful and prosperous life.

Crack the code of Becoming a lifetime millionaire

Leveraging Opportunities for Wealth Creation

Having a clear vision for your financial goals is vital for wealth building. However, having a vision is not enough; you must also be able to discover and capitalize on prospects for wealth development. Here's where strategic planning comes in.

Aligning your vision with strategic planning allows you to identify and capitalize on possible growth areas. This necessitates a proactive mindset, one that is constantly on the lookout for methods to increase your wealth.

Strategic planning include monitoring market trends, evaluating risks and rewards, and making informed decisions based on that information. With a clear vision and strategic planning in place, you can make sound decisions and turn possibilities into long-term success.

Creating riches involves more than simply hard effort. To capitalize on chances for growth and success, a visionary attitude and strategic planning are required. Keep your eyes open and devoted to your vision, and you'll be on your road to building long-term wealth.

Maintaining Momentum and Long-term Success
A one-time action plan is insufficient for creating long-term wealth. It takes consistency to connect one's activities with their vision. Individuals can stay motivated and maintain momentum toward their long-term goals by examining their financial goals on a frequent basis and constantly modifying their vision.

To maintain momentum, it is critical to recognize tiny victories along the way, since they serve as optimistic indicators of progress. It is also critical to maintain discipline in sticking to plans, especially in the face of obstacles or setbacks.

Creating riches through vision necessitates an adaptable and growth-oriented mindset. By viewing setbacks as chances to learn and grow, individuals may refine and reinforce their vision, laying a better basis for long-term success.

Aligning Actions and Vision for Financial Success
One of the keys to accomplishing financial objectives is to continually connect actions and vision. This entails establishing both short-term and long-term goals that contribute to an overarching vision, as well as strategizing and carrying out plans to achieve those objectives.

A clear and well-defined vision helps motivate people to stay focused on their goals and take meaningful steps toward them. Individuals who match their daily actions with their vision can generate enormous momentum that propels them to achievement.

Developing riches via vision necessitates ongoing growth and improvement. To maintain momentum and achieve long-term success, individuals must remain adaptable and committed to their vision, especially when confronted with difficulties or problems. By doing so, people can secure a better financial future for themselves and their loved ones.

Conclusion

In conclusion, the value of vision in wealth creation cannot be emphasized. A clear vision can act as a powerful motivator, providing direction and purpose as people work toward their financial goals.

Individuals who recognize that vision is an important component of wealth building can begin to take meaningful measures toward achievement. A clear vision can help people overcome challenges and hurdles while also discovering and grabbing possibilities for growth and financial benefit.

Furthermore, by cultivating a visionary mentality and continually connecting their activities with their goal, people can maintain momentum and achieve long-term success in wealth creation.

Finally, whether generating wealth through strategic planning or developing a vision-driven approach, clarity of vision is essential for achieving financial success and fulfillment.

Key Takeaways
A clear and appealing vision is essential for wealth generation.
Vision provides concentration, drive, and clarity when achieving financial goals.
Having a clear vision can aid in strategic planning and discovering wealth-building opportunities.

Adapting and evolving one's vision is critical for long-term success in wealth accumulation.

Consistently aligning actions with the vision is critical for maintaining momentum and attaining financial success.

Understanding Wealth Creation.

Creating money is a process that entails defining specific financial goals and working hard to achieve them. Whether you want to start a business, invest in the stock market, or save money, having a clear goal and plan of action is critical to financial success.

CHAPTER 3

SETTING "SMART" FINANCIAL GOALS.

Setting financial wise goals is essential for accomplishing your financial objectives, whether you want to pay off your credit card debt, save for retirement, or concentrate on another financial goal. SMART financial goal setting transforms imprecise aspirations into tangible plans. Instead of saying "I want to pay off my debt" or "I want to save money for the future," it's about setting specific goals like "I will pay off $5,000 in credit card debt this year" or "I will save $1,000 for a family vacation next Christmas." Suddenly, broad-stroke hopes are reshaped and put into action.

How To Set SMART Financial Goals
The acronym SMART stands for Specific, Measurable, Attainable, Realistic, and Timely. Whether you're searching for short-term wins or creating long-term personal finance plans, merely using the SMART objectives template will increase your chances of success. Here's a step-by-step guide to each of its key letters.

1. Make your goals specific.
The first stage is to be specific about your goal. This is always crucial, particularly for high goals like saving a million dollars. Without specifics on how and when those seven figures will be deposited into the bank, a broad scheme like that is doomed to fail.

Creating a precise aim involves a two-pronged strategy. First, decide what you want and how much of it you desire. You may desire to save money, build an emergency fund, or pay off debt; the amount should be concrete. Second, you need to understand why you're doing this. This may not sound like a huge thing, but it is crucial.

Ask yourself, "What is my specific goal, and why is it important that I achieve it?"

SMART Goals

A specific aim could be to save $5,000 this year for an emergency fund (the what) in case your roof has to be repaired or to help you avoid using credit cards. Giving your goal a personal meaning will help you stay focused. If you're unsure about the numbers, conduct some study and make an educated approximation. What's most important is having a clear plan for getting started. You can always adjust your estimate later!

2. Create measurable goals.

Measurable goals are straightforward to track since they are explicit from the outset. When your goals are measurable, you can set checkpoints along the route to show you're making progress. For example, if you want to save $8,000 in a year, you can set a midpoint goal of at least $4,000 after six months. You can even create daily goals. Since there are 365 days in a year, saving just $22 for all 365 days will result in $8,030!

Ask yourself: Is there a simple way to track my progress toward accomplishing this goal?

Matching your checkpoints to your pay cycle will help you save even more money by automating the tedious work. Whatever you do, having a tangible number to deal with will make quantifying your progress simple and, perhaps, even enjoyable. You'll always know how you're doing and whether you need to make any adjustments along the road.

3. Motivate yourself with attainable, action-oriented goals.
Now that you have clear financial goals, you must put your strategy into action. For example, if your objective is to save $100 every month to either pay off credit card debt or put into a summer vacation fund. Where will you acquire the money to pay off $100 of credit card debt, or where will you find $100 in cash for your summer vacation? Will you save the money in a savings account or apply it to your debt straight away?

Ask yourself, "Is my goal attainable?" Is my action plan to achieve it reasonable?

Only you can determine whether your financial goal is feasible and plan the steps you need to take to reach it. Perhaps saving $100 each month is achievable if you pack your lunch four days a week, adhere to a lower entertainment budget, or put your credit cards away for the year to avoid frivolous spending. If you're having problems deciding on an attainable objective for yourself, adapt it to your circumstances. Instead of saving $100 per month, try spending 50% less on eating out or other expenses. Consider any potential impediments that could throw you off path, and make backup plans just in case.

4. Keep your goals realistic.

Setting a realistic financial goal entails being certain that you can achieve it. On the other hand, relying on a surprise inheritance or winning the lottery to fulfill your financial goals is likely to lead to disappointment. Remember that many long-term goals, such as saving a million dollars, will appear unachievable when you are just getting started. However, breaking down these large marathons into tiny sprints can have a significant impact on your thinking. For example, you could set a goal to save as much as possible this month, and then attempt to save even more the next month. Each checkpoint you complete will bring you one step closer to your goal.

Ask yourself if your goals and action plans are feasible. Do I need to break down larger goals into smaller, more manageable ones?

More ways to fix unrealistic financial goals.

5. Maintain Focus with Timely Goals.

You understand what your precise goal is, how to track your progress, how you will attain it, and whether it is reasonable. Now is time to set a deadline. After all, asking oneself to accomplish something "as soon as possible" may take you down a winding, never-ending route to nowhere.

Ask yourself: Does my objective have a realistic timetable that will help me stay focused?

When setting your goals, sit down with a pen and paper and go over all of your objectives. You may wind up with a mix of tasks to complete within one year (short-term), two to five years (medium-term), and more than five years (long-term). After you've identified a few goals, incorporate them into your monthly budget and analyze your progress to see how they fit into your daily life. At the end of each month, evaluate your progress and determine whether any changes or adjustments are required as you move forward.

CHAPTER 4

BUDGETING FOR SUCCESS

One of the most effective modest actions people can take to manage their money is to create (and stick to) a budget. Budgeting is an essential component of financial planning, and without one, it is difficult to manage other parts of personal finance such as credit, insurance, saving, investing, and accomplishing goals like a new automobile or a happy retirement. Financial goals cannot be met if no funds are set aside for them.

Budgeting has also been linked to improved health and financial outcomes in studies. People who budget their money may be more likely to "budget" their calories by self-restricting their food consumption and/or adjusting their physical activity to stay under their daily calorie "allowance."

Here are nine important things to know about budgeting:

The goal is to have positive cash flow. A budget is a plan for future income and expenses, which includes savings. The goal is positive cash flow, which means revenue exceeds savings. A budget, whether handwritten or computer-generated, should have clear sections for revenue, spending, and monetary amounts.

Individual Needs and Wants are Important- Examples include whether you have a stable income (the same amount in each paycheck) or a variable income that varies every month, and whether you like to utilize a "paper and pencil" worksheet, an Excel spreadsheet, or a budgeting app.

Savings is a Fixed Expense- The amount you need to save each month or per paycheck to fund future aspirations should be budgeted as a fixed expense that does not change from month to month. A general online financial goal-setting calculator can help you calculate the appropriate amount to save.

Budgeting Methods Vary- Many people use the same budget format year after year, adjusting for changes in income and expenses. For example, they may use computer applications or apps, as well as a blank sheet of paper. What matters most is that you have a budget, not how you set it.

COVID-19 has had an impact on budget priorities, as many individuals are working less (or not at all) and struggling to make ends meet. Others are earning the same or more than before, and they are saving more as their home expenses have decreased. In either situation, budgets must be changed to reflect changes in cash flow.

Unexpected Expenses Always Occur- It is not a matter of "if," but "when," unexpected expenses occur. For this reason, financial experts recommend inserting a "fudge factor" (also known as a "miscellaneous budget category") in household budgets. If the funds are not required, they can be rolled over into savings.

Expenses Can Be Reduced- Experts advocate beginning with variable expenses like heating/cooling, subscriptions, streaming fees, and food.

Also, look for less expensive shopping options (e.g., thrift stores), cook more at home, and think about methods to cut fixed expenses like refinancing a home mortgage, choosing a less expensive apartment or automobile, and shopping around for insurance discounts.

People who are struggling financially can get public benefits (for example, utility help or food from a food bank) if their income qualifies. This frees up funds for other expenses. Other ways to improve revenue include bartering products instead of spending money and selling unwanted items.

Budgets Affect Credit Scores- By adding debt repayment funds as a fixed item, a budget can help to avoid unfavorable credit report data. A budget, when followed, can also help avoid overspending on credit, lowering a credit cardholder's credit utilization ratio, which accounts for around 30% of a FICO credit score. Finally, a budget can include cash for emergency savings, making it less likely that people will use credit in an emergency.

To construct your own personal budget, follow these two steps. To begin, track your income and expenses for a month or two to obtain reliable information about your current situation.

The characteristics of Successful budgeting

Do you understand how crucial a budget is in running a successful business? A budget is an estimate of income and expenditures for a specific time period. This is a financial document. It keeps track of past expenses and forecasts future income from them. It contributes to the achievement of any enterprise's financial goals. A well-planned, adaptable, and practical budget is essential for business success.

All financial strategies are successful because of effective budgeting. From daily spending to operating a global corporation, a good, realistic, adaptable, and well-designed budget is essential.

The primary characteristics of an effective budget are:

1. It needs to be well-planned and realistic.
It should cover any company's short- and long-term strategies. It should focus on the enterprise's goal. A well-planned and sensible budget is always manageable. It should incorporate all types of long and short-term strategies and expenses in a reasonable manner.

2. It should be flexible.
A flexible budget is usually successful. To carry out the plans and achieve the objectives, a budget must be flexible. A flexible budget is always useful since it allows you to adjust your plans based on demand.

3. It should inspire and motivate.
If a budget can motivate personnel in an enterprise, it can help the company achieve its goals. An exciting budget can boost an enterprise's financial performance. It can also help boost the company's overall performance.

4. It should have diverse plans.
A successful budget should contain both short-term and long-term financial plans. The budget should be created two months ahead of the fiscal year. Long-term plans should last at least three years and be completed every quarter.

A effective budget is critical to the success of any business, organization, or entrepreneur. It demonstrates an action plan that prepares the road for the organization to plan and execute expenses. A successful budget requires the active collaboration of the entire organization.

4. It must convey a sense of ownership.
A successful budget should demonstrate a sense of ownership. It is crucial for the business. It should be presented in accordance with the company's standard performance. A budget should be very acceptable.

5. It should be coordinated.
A successful budget should be well-coordinated. It should work seamlessly across an organization's many units. To build an integrated plan, all different budgets should be combined into the main budget.

6. It should have an excellent representation.
It should accurately reflect the agenda and expenditures. An erroneous budget forces the employee to create budgetary slack. Budgetary slack is the process of diminishing revenue while increasing expenses.
It cannot be endorsed by management or employees. It is expressed monetary or quantitatively in the budget.

7. It should track expenses.
A well-designed budget always keeps track of its spending. It must contain a flawless tracking app. A budget worksheet assists the company in obtaining resources and directing its operations. Analysis of costs, revenue, and taxes clarifies a budget, resulting in its performance and profitability.

8. It should be flexible.
A budget should be flexible. A flexible budget can readily help the firm achieve its aims. However, a tight budget will not help the organization reach its goals. Any modifications must be welcomed in a flexible manner. A tight budget cannot be functional.

9. It should have an appropriate number of spending categories.
A successful budget should accurately reflect the worth of spending categories. It will enable the company figure out its spending tendencies. It should break down major expenses to demonstrate the flow of money transactions and expenditures.

10. It should classify irregular expenses.
It is difficult to track irregular spending because they are considered routine expenses and only occur once or twice a year. A effective budget should account for the appropriate amount of an enterprise's irregular expenses.

11. It should incorporate savings.
A successful budget should incorporate the quantity of saved. If the budget includes savings as an expense, the corporation can use the savings fund in an emergency.

12. It should have regular reviews.
Budgets are reviewed every two or three months. An enterprise or startup's expenses can climb or fall. A successful budget requires constant review and monitoring.

13. Forecasting requires accuracy.
A successful budget should provide reliable forecasts. It ensures a company's growth. Long-term financial planning requires accurate forecasting.

A successful budget should always encourage all employees to achieve their financial objectives. Budgeting is a collaborative effort, and success is determined by its transparency and efficacy.

SAVING AND INVESTING STRATEGIES

Do you save or spend?

If you choose the former, you're in the majority. According to a 2019 Charles Schwab survey, approximately 59% of Americans consider themselves savers. In contrast, more recent studies show that 63% of respondents in a similar cohort are already living paycheck to paycheck.

Clearly, there is a gap between the financial goals we make and the actions we take to achieve them.

Many of us are taught from a young age that saving is the most straightforward way to accumulate wealth and achieve financial independence. But this is a myth. While saving is essential for achieving both goals, making wise financial decisions makes them far more feasible.

Most individuals are afraid of losing money when they invest, which is understandable. When we work hard and are disciplined enough to avoid spending and save, the prospect of losing our hard-earned money makes us uneasy. As a result, we keep our money in an FDIC-insured bank account.

Here's the issue: the money we deposit into our accounts is practically certain to lose value. The low interest rates offered by savings accounts cannot even keep up with inflation, so the purchase value of our money falls as we save longer.

There is some good news, however. If you make sound decisions and invest in the correct locations, you can reduce risk, improve reward, and earn meaningful returns without feeling like you'd be better off in Vegas.

Why should you invest?
Saving versus investing is a frequently debated topic in financial circles.

Saving is an essential component of the financial arsenal for growing wealth – not because it generates wealth on its own, but because it provides the funds required to invest. At the very least, investing allows you to keep up with the cost-of-living increases caused by inflation. The ability to compound interest, or growth earned on growth, is the most significant advantage of a long-term investment strategy.

How much should you save versus invest?
Given that each investor enters the market for different reasons, the best answer to how much you should save is "as much as possible." As a general rule, saving 20% of your income is a good place to start. More is always preferable, but I feel that 20% allows you to accumulate a significant amount of cash over your career.

Initially, you'll want to use these savings to create an emergency fund equivalent to three to six months' worth of regular costs. Once you've saved for emergencies, invest any surplus funds that aren't being used for specific short-term costs.

This capital has the potential to multiply if invested intelligently and over time.

How does investing work?

The market is a place where you can buy and sell stocks, bonds, and other assets. Do not enter the market using your bank account.

You must first open an investing account, similar to a brokerage account, and fund it with cash before purchasing stocks, bonds, and other investable assets.

Stocks vs. bonds: Publicly traded corporations use the market to raise funds for operations, growth, or expansion by issuing stocks (small shares of the company) or bonds (debt).

When a firm offers bonds on the market, it is essentially asking investors for loans to fund its operations. Investors buy the bonds, and the corporation repays them over time, plus a percentage of interest.

Stocks, on the other hand, are tiny amounts of stock in a corporation. When a corporation changes from private to public, its stock can be purchased and sold on the open market, indicating that it is no longer privately owned. A stock price is generally representative of the company's value, but the actual price is determined by what market players are ready to pay or accept on any particular day.

Other types of investments
You aren't confined to stocks and bonds, however. You can purchase...

Because of their price volatility, stocks are viewed as riskier investments than bonds. If bad news about a firm emerges, consumers may be willing to pay less to buy shares than they were previously, lowering the stock price. If you paid a high amount for the stock, you risk losing it if it falls in value.

Stocks are also riskier because when companies fail, bondholders receive their money back, whereas stockholders do not have this guarantee.

Making (and losing) money: In the market, the purchase and sale price of whatever you buy determines whether you make or lose money. If you buy a stock at $10 and sell it at $15, you'll make $5. If you buy at $15 and sell at $10, you'll lose $5. Gains and losses are only "realized" or tallied when the asset is sold — so the stock you bought for $10 may fall to $6, but you would only "lose" $4 if you sell it for $6. Maybe you wait a year and then sell the stock when it reaches $11, earning $1 per share.

Are your investments reasonable?
Now that you understand how to invest, determine where you want to put your money.
Remember that the best risk an investor can take is one that is well-thought-out.

But, how can you be calculated? How do you tell the difference between a wise and a risky investment? Truthfully, "smart" and "risky" are relative to each investor. Your circumstances (e.g., age, debt level, family status) or risk tolerance can help you determine where you fit on the risk spectrum.

Younger investors with several years till retirement should have riskier portfolios. That extended time horizon allows investors more years to weather the market's ups and downs — and during their working years, investors should ideally be adding to their investment accounts rather than withdrawing money.

Someone approaching or in retirement, on the other hand, is far more exposed to market fluctuations. If you utilize an investment account to meet your living needs, you may be forced to withdraw the funds during a market downturn, resulting in not only a smaller portfolio but also large investment losses.

A higher-risk portfolio is likely to have a large number of equities and few (if any) bonds. As youthful investors age and need to reduce risk in their portfolios, they should cut their stock investments while increasing their bond investments.

The ebb and flow of life will have a greater impact on your finances than you may imagine. Being realistic about your present financial situation will help you make sound investment decisions.

Are you creating money that will last?
Larger-than-average profits nearly usually necessitate higher-than-average risks, and there are no free lunches in investing. As you seek to develop wealth and safeguard your financial future, stay focused on three long-term investment requirements:

Create a "just in case" nest egg: Nearly 25% of Americans have no emergency savings. Don't get ensnared in that trap. Retirement savings accounts are important savings vehicles, but withdrawing them before retirement often results in high tax penalties. To avoid this, as previously said, create an emergency fund equal to three to six months' worth of living expenses.

One of the most important things you can do for your financial future is to set up automatic savings – that is, have your bank direct a percentage of your paycheck to a savings account. This guarantees that you save consistently rather than forcing you to make a conscious decision to put money aside.

This quantity should be kept in a low-risk location, such as a bank account, and it should be liquid (i.e., cash or something else that is constantly available to you) so that you can access it if necessary. Once you've set up an emergency fund, invest future savings based on your risk tolerance.

Steer your savings in the appropriate direction: In general, you should begin by determining what percentage of your assets you want to be riskier (stocks/shares) and what percentage you want to be safer (cash and bonds). As previously said, this is determined by your risk tolerance. Someone who is young and working should invest almost entirely in stocks, whereas someone nearing retirement age should allocate more funds to bonds.

If you're just getting started investing, I recommend mutual funds or ETFs (a collection of stocks, bonds, and other investment vehicles) over individual stocks (ownership in only one company) because it'll be easier to create a diversified account with funds if the account is small. Diversification (holding a variety of assets) is crucial because it reduces the likelihood that your entire portfolio will lose value during a market downturn. You'll want to look for funds with a proven track record and moderate fees.

When you're ready to start investing in individual stocks, you'll want to conduct the same type of research on any firms you're considering: Do they have a solid track record? Do they have effective management? Is the stock's pricing reasonable? Does it diversify your portfolio, or is it similar to what you already own? Spend some time on this phase to ensure you make sound financial decisions.

Make variation a theme of your investments: Diversifying your whole financial "portfolio" (i.e., all of the investments you own) is crucial to wealth creation since it allows you to better manage risk. Stocks are one of the most popular investments, but you don't want to base your entire financial future on the performance of a single firm — or even a larger market.

Depending on your financial situation and risk tolerance, you may want to investigate investing in private equity, venture capital, precious metals, commodities, and real estate, all of which are now available on the market. All of these assets can help you diversify your portfolio and manage risk.

Why? Because they rely on different fundamental causes. This implies they generally behave in ways that are uncorrelated with one another and with more traditional investments such as stocks and bonds, so they may rise while equities fall.

A well-constructed portfolio should comprise a variety of assets (stocks, bonds, etc.) that do not move in tandem. This minimizes portfolio volatility without necessarily diminishing return possibilities.

While these methods will not provide you with complete financial independence, I feel they are an excellent beginning point. They can help you save money, diversify your portfolio, and begin creating wealth for a better financial future.

CHAPTER 5

ENTREPRENEURSHIP AND WEALTH CREATION

Starting a small business is a unique decision made by each owner for their own personal reasons. Understanding their genuine purpose for beginning their business frequently necessitates asking multiple questions, but it all boils down to earning money and building wealth.

In that regard, entrepreneurship is a great wealth-building instrument since it allows for the development of endless money while also providing individuals with some degree of autonomy and self-determination over their life. This chapter will explore the key ideas that drive wealth growth through entrepreneurship.

Paths for Wealth Creation
Creating money should be considered as a lifelong journey rather than a single event, and it can be accomplished by pursuing one of four basic paths.
These options include inheriting wealth, saving and investing, pursuing a lucrative career, or starting your own business. Each path presents unique opportunities and difficulties that influence the quantity of wealth accumulated and the time required to accomplish so.

Entrepreneurship is regarded as one of the most effective paths to wealth generation. It is open to people of various ages, education levels, and demographics. A company's value can rise dramatically over time, resulting in the acquisition of huge wealth. However, there are hazards associated with entrepreneurship, including financial risk and the likelihood of business failure.

Woman jumping in front of a graph depicting the steps of entrepreneurship, beginning with an idea and progressing to success. Entrepreneurship is a viable means of generating income. Realistically, entrepreneurship involves the danger of financial and business failure.

Wealth Creation: Begin with the End in Mind.
Most books and articles on entrepreneurship state that the first step is idea generating. However, anyone considering beginning a new firm should first consider and define their wealth goals and objectives.

As an entrepreneur, creating wealth entails establishing a productive business that creates income for the owner while increasing in value over time. This can be accomplished by increasing profits and selling the business or shares for a large profit. It is critical to define your business expectations, such as whether it will be a side hustle or full-time, how much income is required to support your personal budget, and whether it will generate wealth beyond living expenses for future investments such as purchasing a home, funding retirement, or paying for your children's college tuition.

Once you've identified your wealth goals, you'll have a baseline for determining the fiscal sustainability of your new business idea.

Idea Generation and Validation

Developing a viable company idea entails more than a spontaneous thinking or just turning a passion into a business. It entails carefully finding a market gap and comprehending potential clients' wants and preferences. The most common error a new business owner may make is attempting to sell a product or service without fully understanding the target market's needs, preferences, and readiness to buy.

Once you've developed an idea, you must validate it. Validation necessitates market research to ensure that your product or service generates enough income and profit to fulfill the entrepreneur's financial goals and objectives.

One goldfish jumping out of a bowl to show the need for business managers to go beyond their
If entrepreneurs understand the fishbowl phenomena, they will be able to properly assess the viability of their ideas.
Don't fall victim to the Fish in the Fishbowl phenomenon.
Imagine a little fish in a fishbowl. The fishbowl depicts the market in which a small business operates, while the fish represents the company itself. The water in the bowl represents the resources accessible to the business, including as capital, talent, and customers, all of which are limited by the size of the fishbowl.

Interestingly, the fish does not recognize he is in a fishbowl. Looking through the glass, the fish perceives the entire room as his habitat, despite the fact that his universe is defined solely by the boundaries of the fishbowl. A fish can only grow as much as its fishbowl allows, and a tiny business can only sell as much as its market requires. To survive, the fish may require a wider environment than what is provided in its bowl. Similarly, a company may need to assess whether the proposed business idea is actually limited to a local market or if there are opportunities for other markets or broadening its products in order to continue growing.

The fish in a fishbowl analogy effectively depicts the problems and opportunities that an entrepreneur must examine before starting a new business. Like fish, firms must adapt to their surroundings, manage resources intelligently, and deal with the consequences of market limits. Understanding the fishbowl effect allows potential business owners to better assess the viability of their ideas.

Aligning Business and Personal Wealth Goals

The great majority of micro-small business owners don't have a business plan, and many don't even have well-prepared financial predictions. Some take satisfaction in "flying by the seat of their pants." However, data on small business failure show that a
a well-structured business plan is critical to long-term business success and sustainability.

However, for the entrepreneur to profit from the firm, the business plan must be in line with the owner's own financial aspirations and ambitions. The plan outlines your business objectives, strategies for accomplishing them, and the resources needed. A strong business plan contains market study, financial estimates, and an operational plan.

Balancing Business and Personal Financial Health.

A critical component of establishing financial success through entrepreneurship is ensuring that the business can scale and grow beyond generating only enough income to support the owner's family. Any business's growth and scalability should be guided by adequate planning, including a capital budgeting plan. Every year, a number of small firms go bankrupt due to unplanned or unanticipated growth. My father once told me, "An opportunity is only an opportunity if you are in a position to take it."

Obtaining finance is critical for any organization to meet its growth goals. Capital readiness is planning for and addressing the financial health of both the firm and the owner. If the owner's financial situation is unstable, it might have a detrimental impact on the financial health of the business, and vice versa. Finally, acquiring a business loan requires rigorous capital planning and administration to accomplish the required growth and success.

Conclusion

Entrepreneurship is a significant tool for generating money. However, it only works when idea generation results in an economically viable company model, which is backed by strong business planning, capital acquisition and structure, managed execution, planned growth, and reinvestment. While the path is difficult, the potential rewards are substantial. Understanding and using these essential concepts will allow you to leverage the power of entrepreneurship to generate significant riches.

NAVIGATING THE ENTREPRENEUR'S JOURNEY

Entrepreneurial Journey
When it comes to making their ideas a reality, first-time entrepreneurs sometimes find themselves at a crossroads of ingenuity and inexperience. Similarly, seasoned industry professionals who are caught in dying industries as a result of technological developments may have a plethora of industry expertise but lack the know-how to drive market transformation. Both scenarios necessitate the expertise of seasoned entrepreneurs who have successfully brought products or services to market.

Learn from the best.

As a new entrepreneur, the first step is to educate yourself by reading books and watching films about successful entrepreneurs and business leaders. Recognizing that even the most successful brands faced early challenges as they created their route. There are no shortcuts to experience, but learning from people who have gone through the ups and downs offers essential insights.

Passion's Blind Spots and the Need to monetize Your Vision

One of the main areas where entrepreneurs frequently get stuck is their enthusiasm for their new idea. Passion is crucial, but it must be balanced with a strategic approach. A lack of experience or an unwillingness to understand the market clearly can be harmful. Productivity and monetization are the keys to scalability and sustainability. It is critical to recognize that this venture cannot be viewed as a hobby if the goal is to develop a true, profitable corporation.

Embracing failure and cultivating resilience

A resilient mindset is critical in the entrepreneurial path. You must be prepared to fail, pick yourself up, and persevere until you attain your goal. Setbacks are unavoidable on the way to success, and the ability to endure in the face of these hurdles distinguishes successful entrepreneurs. This path requires a mindset capable of enduring the inevitable ups and downs.

The Business Plan Blueprint

To negotiate the complexity of converting ideas into successful businesses, entrepreneurs need a strategic roadmap. The accompanying Business Plan Blueprint is the foundation for success, providing a disciplined framework for translating your vision into an actionable plan. From the succinct summary offered in the Executive Summary to the extensive analysis of the Market, Organization, and Product or Service Line, each part is critical in designing the launch of your business. With a focus on Monetization Strategy, Marketing and Sales, Funding Request, Financial Projections, and Seeking Guidance, this blueprint outlines the essential elements that lay the groundwork for a comprehensive business plan, providing entrepreneurs with a simple guide to success in today's rapidly changing marketplace.

1. Executive Summary:
A brief explanation of your company's concept, objective, and vision.

A snapshot of major milestones, objectives, funding requirements, and financial estimates.

2. Business Description:
Legal structure, location, and history of your company.
Unique selling point (USP) and how your company meets market needs.

3. Market Analysis:
In-depth examination of the target market, including size, demographics, and trends. Assessment of rivals and methods for differentiating your firm. Marketing and sales strategy.

4. Organization and management:
Roles and expertise of important team members, as well as the organizational structure.
Introducing any advisory board or mentors.

5. Product/Service Line:
Provide a detailed description of your offering.
Highlight your intellectual property or proprietary features.
Development stage and future ambitions.

6. Monetisation Strategy:
Clearly explain how you intend to monetise your product or service.
Discuss scalability and sustainability with effective monetization.

7. Marketing and sales:
Strategies for reaching your target customer.
Pricing strategy and sales forecasts.

8. Funding request:
The amount of funding sought and how it is allocated (for example, equipment, marketing, and working capital). Timeline for extra financial requirements.

9. Financial projections:
Detailed financial projections, including revenue, balance, and cash flow figures.
Breakeven analysis and critical financial metrics.

10. Seeking guidance:
Engage mentors or business experts to provide continuing support.
Update your business plan on a regular basis as your venture grows and changes.

In conclusion.
Finally, you are responsible for the success of your entrepreneurial journey. It involves hard work, a realistic mentality, and the capacity to overcome the numerous challenges that will inevitably arise. Accept failure as a stepping stone rather than a stumbling block, and keep moving forward until you attain your goal. Remember that developing a great business is a marathon, not a sprint.

IDENTIFYING BUSINESS OPPORTUNITIES

Although many prospective entrepreneurs begin with a new business idea, the question remains: Is it a viable business opportunity? In other words, does it meet a market demand, alleviate a customer's pain point, or enhance an existing product?

Perhaps you want to see if your business idea is viable, or you enjoy the concept of entrepreneurship and are looking for the appropriate opportunity to get started. In any case, you should become acquainted with many types of business possibilities and learn how to recognize them.

Here are three types of business chances to look for, how to spot them, and how to keep a disruptive attitude for entrepreneurial success.

Types of business opportunities to look for:
1. Jobs to be done.
At its foundation, entrepreneurship is the process of utilizing available resources to meet unmet market demands. One method for identifying those needs is the jobs to be done theory, which holds that individuals do not buy a product; rather, they "hire" it to complete a job.

One example is McDonald's milkshakes. McDonald's management were astonished to learn that milkshake sales were strongest in the morning. Through research, they realized that customers were employing milkshakes to keep them entertained and full throughout their morning travels.

"It enables you to reach out and grab hold of the causal mechanism that drives customers to purchase your product or service." "If we understand the job the customer is trying to do, and then develop a product that nails this job perfectly, the probability that your innovation will be successful is improved in dramatic ways."

This idea also broadens the breadth of the competitive landscape and helps you understand how many options clients have when they need a given job done.

Returning to the milkshake example, customers might have hired faster snacks like bananas or granola bars to do the same job of keeping them filled and Occupied throughout their journeys, even if they were not direct rivals. In this scenario, the milkshake outperformed competition because of its thick consistency, which allowed it to be drunk slowly during commutes.

2. Low-End Market Opportunities
Understanding the disruptive innovation hypothesis is critical for finding market gaps. This idea describes how startups with lower resources might enter existing marketplaces and displace incumbent corporations that own portions of them. Disruptive innovation may be divided into two categories: low-end disruption and new market disruption.
Low-end disruption happens when a new market entry enters the lowest sector using a low-profit business model. Entering at the bottom of the

market ensures that the incumbent company has no financial incentive to fight back; after all, it holds the most profitable segments.

Over time, the new entrant advances to the next highest market sector. Once again, the incumbent corporation is financially driven to exit that segment and transition to higher-profit ones. This will continue until the new entrant has totally driven the existing company out of the market.

This technique is more effective than directly competing with the incumbent company for top market segments because the latter is more likely to defend its position.

3. New market opportunities.
The second sort of disruptive innovation is new-market disruption. It offers numerous opportunities for entrepreneurial success, so it's critical to understand how to discover it.

When a corporation creates a new segment within an existing market, it causes new market disruption. This new market frequently caters to customers who are overserved by existing services, which means they are unwilling to pay for the most recent features of the incumbent company's products.

If you see such an opportunity, build a product that is less expensive and of "good enough" quality to establish and capture a new market segment.

The transistor radio, introduced into the personal entertainment industry by Texas Instruments in 1954, is one example of new-market disruption. The portable radio catered to young, non-wealthy individuals who were overserved by other radio products of the time, which were enormous, expensive, and made to sit in houses like furniture. Texas Instruments opened the way for higher-quality options, such as the Sony Walkman and Apple iPod, by developing a low-cost, "good enough" option for listening to music, eventually rendering in-home radio consoles obsolete.

Identifying overserved people in any market allows you to identify and capitalize on opportunities.

3 Ways to Identify Business Opportunities
With a solid awareness of the different types of possibilities available, you may begin spotting them. Here are three approaches you can use, along with examples to help you learn.

1. Identify your pain points.
When looking for possible market demands, begin with yourself. What processes or duties do you find bothersome in your daily life? What is the task at hand for which you have yet to find the ideal product?

Many great entrepreneurial ventures started with a personal issue in the founder's life. For example, when Neil Blumenthal lost his prescription glasses and couldn't afford to replace them, he founded Warby Parker, an eyewear firm that sells affordable, fashionable glasses.

Starting with personal questions might assist establish if others are experiencing the same pain point and whether opportunities are low-end or new-market disruptors.

2. Conduct Market Research.
Conducting market research is another approach to determine the viability of a company proposal. This includes conducting industry research to describe the competitive environment and identify your target audience, as well as interviewing or surveying individuals who meet your target demographics.

Observing and getting input from real people allows you to think about their viewpoints and gain a better grasp of their motivations, frustrations, concerns, and ambitions. This might assist you determine whether your product satisfies a need and the size of the potential audience.

Once an opportunity has been found, you may use design thinking to create an innovative solution that meets the needs identified through research.

How to Conduct Market Research for Startups

Every creative product idea raises the pressing question: "Will people want to buy it?""

As an entrepreneur with a huge concept, how can you effectively predict how potential buyers will react to your product? Market research can provide the information needed to determine whether your product is a good fit for your target audience.
Before starting a new business, you need understand market research. Here's how to perform market research for a company and why it matters.

What is market research?
Market research is the process of acquiring information about customers and the whole market in order to assess the viability of a product or service. Interviews, surveys, focus groups, and industry data analysis are all forms of market research.

The purpose of market research is to gain a deeper understanding of potential customers, how effectively your product or service meets their needs, and how it compares to competing offerings.

There are two sorts of research to conduct: primary and secondary.

Primary research entails gathering data to understand about your individual clients or target market category. It's useful for developing buyer personas, segmenting your market, and enhancing your product to meet your customers' wants.

Secondary research is done using data that you did not acquire yourself. Industry publications, public databases, and proprietary data from other companies can all help you learn more about your target market segment and industry.

WHY IS MARKET RESEARCH IMPORTANT TO ENTREPRENEURS?

Before beginning your business, undertake market research to ensure that your product or service will be well-received. Feedback from people in your target demographic can be quite useful as you develop and enhance your product.

Market research can also assist you decide on a price plan by assessing customers' willingness to pay for your goods. Additionally, it helps improve the user experience by identifying which elements are most important to potential customers.

When deciding which firms to support, investors prioritize detailed market research that demonstrates intriguing potential. Providing physical proof that your product meets a market demand, as well as demonstrating that you've spent the time iterating and improving it, indicate that your startup may be a worthy investment.

How to Conduct Market Research for Startups

1. Form hypotheses.

What questions are you hoping to solve through market research? Using these questions, you can create predictions known as hypotheses.

Defining your assumptions upfront can assist guide your approach to subject selection, research questions, and testing strategies.

One such question you could ask is, "How much are people in my target demographic willing to pay for the current version of my product?" Your hypothesis could be: "If my product includes all of its current features, customers will be willing to pay $500 for it."

Another example question you could ask is, "What is the user's biggest pain point, and does my product meet their needs?" Your hypothesis could be: "I believe the user's biggest pain point is a simple, unintimidating way to learn basic car maintenance, and I predict that my product will meet that need."

You can and should test numerous hypotheses, but attempt to limit the number per test to keep the research focused.

2. Select the type of research required to test hypotheses.
After you've developed your hypothesis, decide what type of study to do.

If your hypotheses are centered on determining your startup's position in the larger market, begin with secondary research. This can entail analyzing existing data to assess market size, how much of that market your firm could feasibly hold, who your main competitors are, and how your brand and product stack up against them.

If your hypotheses necessitate primary research, determine which data collection method is ideal for your purposes. These may include one-on-one interviews, surveys, focus groups, and polls. Primary research provides insights into consumer satisfaction and loyalty, brand recognition and perception, and real-time product usability.

3. Identify the target demographics and recruit subjects
To acquire useful insights, you must first understand your target population. Are you want to cater to working parents, young athletes, or pet owners? Determine who might benefit from your product.

Primary research requires subject recruitment. Several strategies may be used to achieve this, such as:

Word-of-mouth is the easiest but least reliable method of recruiting people. Ask people you know to recommend others as study subjects, and then screen them to ensure they suit your desired demographic.

Promoting the study via social media: Many social media platforms allow you to target ads to people who fit specific demographics or interests. This allows you to reach out to a big number of people who qualify.

Hiring a third-party market research company: Some organizations offer full market research services, including participant recruitment and research on your behalf.
Regardless of how you recruit participants, make sure they complete a screener survey beforehand. This will help you to evaluate whether they fit the exact demographic you want to study or have a feature that removes them from the research pool. It also includes demographic information, such as age and color, allowing you to choose a diverse subset of your target market.

In addition, you can provide incentives for involvement, such as money, meal coupons, gift cards, or early access to your product. Make it clear that reward is intended to show appreciation for the subjects' time and honest input.

4. Conduct the Research.
Conduct your research once you've decided on the type of study and target demographic that will be used to test your hypothesis. To reduce bias, ask someone who is unfamiliar with your hypotheses to conduct interviews or lead focus groups.

Ask questions tailored to your audience and hypotheses. For example, if you want to assess existing customers' purchasing motivations, you may ask: "What problem were you attempting to solve when you first purchased the product?"'

When studying brand perception, your target audience should be potential buyers who are unfamiliar with your brand. Present them with a list of competitor logos, including yours, and ask them to rank the companies based on perceived reliability.

While the questions you ask are intended to verify or disprove hypotheses, be sure they do not lead subjects in one direction. To create fair research questions, utilize neutral wording and change the order of the answers in multiple-choice questions. If respondents believe the third option is always associated with a specific outcome, they are less likely to select the same option repeatedly. It also helps to account for primacy bias (the tendency to choose the first choice in a list) and recency bias (the tendency to pick the last option in a list).

Once you've acquired the data, make sure it's organized properly and securely so you can preserve the subjects' identities.

5. Gather insights and identify action items.
After organizing your data, evaluate it to gain actionable insights. While some of the data will be qualitative rather than quantitative, you can identify trends in the responses to make it quantifiable. For example, 15 out of 20 individuals reported feeling overwhelmed while attempting to assemble your product.

After you've studied the data and used data visualizations to illustrate emerging trends, create an action plan.
If the majority of consumers in your target demographic reported feeling overwhelmed while constructing your product, action steps could include:

Developing several versions of assembly instructions to test with other groups, including alternative illustrations and instructive language.
Researching best practices for instruction manuals.
Each round of market research provides more information about how potential customers perceive and experience your product.

Market research is an ongoing endeavor.
While conducting market research before releasing your product is beneficial, you should reassess your assumptions and develop new ones as your firm grows.
By performing market research on each version of your product, you can gradually enhance it and ensure that it meets the needs of your target clients.

3. Question Processes
You can also find business opportunities by investigating the processes and delivery methods of existing product or service offerings. Try to analyze each process with an open mind and offer questions about how you could enhance it. For example:

Could this procedure be made faster?
Could this process be carried out with a lower-cost business model?
Is there a more sustainable way to carry out this process?
Does this process exclude any certain groups of people?
If so, is there a way to make the process more accessible to everyone?

To become an entrepreneur, you don't have to reinvent the wheel; all you have to do is see the existing potential for innovation.

LEADING THROUGH A DISRUPTIVE LENS

When looking for company and market prospects, start with a disruptive mindset. You can uncover unmet customer wants and use his disruptive innovation theory to establish whether your product has a low-end or new-market entry point.

Rather than directly challenging corporations that dominate market categories, you might discover people who are over- or underserved by current products and compete on a disruptive level.

CHAPTER 6

Investing wisely

UNDERSTANDING DIFFERENT INVESTMENT VEHICLES

What is Investing ?
In general, investing is the process of putting money to work in a project or activity over time in order to generate positive returns. It is the act of allocating resources, usually capital (money), with the intention of earning income, profit, or gains.
One can invest in a variety of ventures (directly or indirectly), such as utilizing money to start a business, or in assets, such as purchasing real estate with the intention of generating rental revenue and/or selling it for more money down the road.
Investing differs from saving in that the money is put to work, implying that there is an inherent risk that the connected project(s) will fail, resulting in a loss of funds. Investing differs from speculation in that the latter does not put money to work directly, but rather bets on short-term price swings.

In investment, risk and return are inextricably linked; low risk typically equates to low predicted profits, whereas larger returns are usually associated with higher risk. Basic investments, such as Certificates of Deposit (CDs), are low-risk; bonds or fixed-income instruments are higher-risk, while stocks or equities are considered riskier. Commodities and derivatives are widely regarded as high-risk investments. One can also invest in something practical, such as land or real estate, as well as delicate objects like fine art and antiques.

Risk and return expectations might vary greatly within the same asset class. A blue chip traded on the New York Stock market, for example, has a considerably different risk-return profile than a micro-cap traded on a smaller market.
An asset's returns vary depending on its nature. For example, many equities pay quarterly dividends, whereas bonds typically pay interest quarterly. Many jurisdictions tax various sources of income at varying rates.

In addition to regular income, such as dividends or interest, price appreciation is a major source of return. The total return on an investment can thus be defined as the sum of income and capital appreciation. According to Standard & Poor's, dividends have generated approximately a third of total equity return for the S&P 500 since 1926, while capital gains have contributed the other two-thirds.
Capital gains are therefore a key aspect of investment.
Savings and investment are viewed by economists as two sides of the same coin.
This is because when you save money by putting it in a bank, the bank lends it to individuals or businesses who want to put it to good use. As a result, your savings are frequently used to fund someone person's investment.

Types of Investment

Today, investing is most commonly linked with financial tools that enable individuals or organizations to raise and deploy cash to firms. These businesses then rake in the funds and use it for expansion or profit-generating operations.

While the universe of investments is enormous, the following are the most prevalent forms of investments:

Stocks

A purchaser of a company's stock becomes a fractional owner of the company. Shareholders are the owners of a company's stock who can participate in its growth and success through stock price appreciation and monthly dividend payments from the company's profits.

Bonds

Bonds are debt liabilities issued by governments, municipalities, and corporations. Purchasing a bond indicates that you own a portion of an entity's debt and are entitled to periodic interest payments and the recovery of the bond's face value when it expires.

Funds

Investment managers administer funds, which allow investors to invest in stocks, bonds, preferred shares, commodities, and other assets. Mutual funds and exchange-traded funds (ETFs) are two of the most frequent fund types. Mutual funds do not trade on an exchange and are valued at the end of the trading day, but ETFs trade on stock exchanges and, like stocks, are valued continuously during the trading day. Mutual funds and ETFs can either passively track indices like the S&P 500 or the Dow Jones Industrial Average, or they can be actively managed by fund managers.

Investment Trusts

Trusts are another form of pooled investing. Real estate investment trusts (REITs) are among the most popular in this category. REITs invest in commercial or residential properties and make regular payouts to their investors from the rental revenue generated by these properties. REITs trade on stock markets, giving their investors the advantage of quick liquidity.

Alternative Investments

Alternative investments are a broad category that encompasses hedge funds and private equity. Hedge funds get their name from the ability to hedge their investment bets by going long and short on stocks and other investments. Private equity allows companies to raise funds without going public. Hedge funds and private equity were generally exclusively available to affluent individuals known as "accredited investors" who met specific income and net worth standards. However, in recent years, alternative investments have been presented in fund structures that are available to regular investors.

Option and Other Derivatives

Derivatives are financial instruments whose value is derived from another asset, such as a stock or index. Options contracts are a common derivative in which the buyer has the right but not the obligation to buy or sell a security at a predetermined price within a specified time frame. Derivatives typically include leverage, making them a high-risk, high-reward proposition.

Commodities

Metals, oil, grain, and animal goods are all examples of commodities, as are financial instruments and currencies. They can be traded via commodity futures, which are contracts to purchase or sell a given quantity of a commodity at a predetermined price on a specific future date, or ETFs. Commodities can be used to hedge risk or to speculate.

Comparing Investment Styles

Let's compare some of the most popular investing styles:

Active versus passive investing: Active investing seeks to "beat the index" by actively managing an investment portfolio. Passive investment, on the other hand, promotes a passive approach, such as purchasing an index fund, in awareness of the difficulty of constantly beating the market. While there are advantages and disadvantages to both approaches, few fund managers regularly outperform their benchmarks, justifying the greater expenses of active management.

Growth versus value: Growth investors want to invest in high-growth companies, which usually have higher valuation ratios like Price-Earnings (P/E) than value companies. Value investors seek out companies with considerably lower PEs and larger dividend yields than growth companies, as they may be out of favor with investors, either temporarily or permanently.

How to Invest?

DIY Investing

The topic of "how to invest" boils down to whether you are a Do-It-Yourself (DIY) investor or want to have your money managed professionally. Many individuals who prefer to manage their own money have accounts with discount or internet brokerages because of the low commissions and simplicity of trading on their platforms.

DIY investing, also known as self-directed investment, needs a certain level of education, expertise, time commitment, and emotional control. If these characteristics do not characterize you well, it may be wise to hire a professional to help you manage your money.

Professionally Managed Investing
Investors who want professional money management typically have wealth managers oversee their investments. Wealth managers typically charge their clients a percentage of the assets under management (AUM) as fees. While professional money management is more expensive than managing money on one's own, some investors are willing to pay for the convenience of delegating research, investing decisions, and trading to a professional.

A Brief History of Investment
While the concept of investing has existed for millennia, its current form can be traced back to the 17th and 18th centuries, when the first public markets were established, connecting individuals with investment possibilities.

Industrial Revolution Investing
The Industrial Revolutions of 1760-1840 and 1860-1914 resulted in increased wealth, which allowed individuals to save and invest, fostering

the development of an advanced banking system. The majority of the established banks that dominate the investment industry date back to the nineteenth century.

20th Century Investments

The twentieth century saw the emergence of new concepts in asset pricing, portfolio theory, and risk management, paving the way for new investment theory. Many new investment vehicles were developed in the second half of the twentieth century, including hedge funds, private equity, venture capital, real estate investment trusts, and exchange traded funds.

In the 1990s, the fast growth of the Internet made online trading and research capabilities available to the general public, completing the century-long democratization of investing.

21st Century Investing

The bursting of the dot.com boom, which spawned a new generation of billionaires through investments in technology-driven and online business stocks, marked the beginning of the twenty-first century and have prepared the ground for the future.

The Great Recession (2007-2009), caused by an overwhelming number of failed investments in mortgage-backed securities, is one of the most noteworthy events of the twenty-first century, if not history. Well-known banks and investment organizations failed, foreclosures increased, and the wealth disparity grew.

The twenty-first century also made investing more accessible to beginners and unorthodox investors by filling the market with bargain online investment businesses and free-trading apps like Robinhood.

Investing vs. speculation.
Three criteria determine whether purchasing an asset is considered speculation or investment:

The level of risk taken on: Investing often carries less risk than speculation.
The investment's holding term: Investing normally requires a longer holding period, which is often measured in years; speculation requires considerably shorter holding periods.
Price appreciation may be a minor component of investment returns, whereas dividends or distributions may play a significant role. In most cases, price appreciation is the primary source of profit in speculating. Given that price volatility is a standard metric of risk, it comes to reason that a stable blue-chip is far less dangerous than a cryptocurrency. Thus, purchasing a dividend-paying blue chip with the intention of owning it for several years qualifies as investment. A trader, on the other hand, who buys a cryptocurrency with the intention of flipping it for a quick profit in a few days is clearly speculative.

Example of Return on Investment
Assume you bought 100 shares of XYZ stock for $310 and sold them exactly one year later for $460.20. Without commissions, what was the approximate total return you received?
Keep in mind that XYZ does not pay stock dividends. The capital gain would be (($460.20 - $310)/$310) multiplied by 100%, which equals 48.5%.

Assume XYZ paid out dividends during your ownership period, and you earned $5 per share. Your estimated overall return would be 50.11% ($500/$31,000) x 100% = 1.61% for dividends and 48.5% for capital gains.

How Do I Start Investing?
You have the option of doing it yourself, selecting investments based on your investing style, or hiring an investment expert, such as an advisor or broker. Before investing, you should identify your preferences and risk tolerance. If you are risk-averse, investing in stocks and options may not be the ideal alternative. Create a strategy that outlines how much to invest, how frequently to invest, and what to invest in based on your goals and priorities. Before allocating your resources, examine the target investment to ensure it is consistent with your plan and has the ability to produce the required results. Remember, you don't need a lot of money to get started, and you may adjust as your needs change.

What are some types of investments?
There are many different kinds of investments available. Stocks, bonds, real estate, and ETFs/mutual funds are among the most popular investments. Other investment options include real estate, CDs, annuities, cryptocurrency, commodities, collectibles, and precious metals.

How Can Investing Help Me Grow Money?
Investing is not just for the wealthy. You can invest in little sums. For example, you can buy low-cost stocks, put tiny sums in an interest-bearing savings account, or save until you reach a certain amount to invest. If your employer provides a retirement plan, such as a 401(k),

start modest and gradually raise your contributions. If your company participates in matching, you may find that your investment has doubled.

You can start investing in stocks, bonds, and mutual funds, or even set up an IRA. Starting with $1,000 is nothing to scoff at. A $1,000 investment in Amazon's 1997 initial public offering would now be worth millions. This was partly owing to multiple stock splits, but it does not change the outcome: massive returns. Most financial organizations provide savings accounts, which often do not demand a big investment. Savings accounts do not normally offer large interest rates; therefore, shop around to locate one with the finest features and competitive rates.

Believe it or not, you can start investing in real estate with just $1,000. You may be unable to purchase an income-producing property, but you can invest in a firm that does. A real estate investment trust (REIT) is a firm that invests and manages real estate to generate profits and revenue. With $1,000, you can buy REIT stocks, mutual funds, or exchange-traded funds.

Is investing the same as gambling?
No, gambling and investing are very different. Investing involves putting your money into projects or activities that are expected to create a favorable return over time. Gambling is placing bets on the outcomes of events or games. Your money is not being put to use at all. Gambling often has a negative expected return. Even if an investment may lose money, this would be because the project failed to deliver. Gambling, on the other hand, is completely random.

The Bottom Line

Investing is the process of transferring resources into something in order to generate income or profit. The type of investment you choose will most likely be determined by your objectives and risk tolerance. Assuming little risk typically generates lesser returns, whereas assuming considerable risk yields higher returns. Stocks, bonds, real estate, precious metals, and other assets are all available for investment. Investing can be done with cash, assets, cryptocurrency, or other forms of payment.

Stocks, bonds, mutual funds, and real estate are all diverse sorts of investment vehicles, with varying amounts of risk and profit.

Investors can invest freely without the assistance of an investment expert or hire a certified and registered investment advisor. Technology has also enabled investors to receive automated investment solutions through roboadvisors.

The quantity of consideration, or money, required to invest is largely determined by the type of investment and the investor's financial situation, needs, and objectives. However, several vehicles have reduced the minimum investment required, allowing more people to participate.

Regardless of how or what you choose to invest in, you should research your target as well as your investment manager or platform.
One of the best pieces of advice from senior and skilled investor, **Warren Buffet is to "never invest in a business you cannot understand."**

KEY TAKEAWAYS

Investing is allocating capital (money) to projects or activities that are projected to yield a favorable return over time.

The sort of returns created varies by project or asset; real estate can generate both rents and capital gains; many stocks offer quarterly dividends; and bonds often pay regular interest.

In investment, risk and return are two sides of the same coin; low risk typically equates to low predicted profits, whereas larger returns are usually associated with higher risk.

Investors can do it themselves or hire a professional money manager. Whether buying a securities is considered investment or speculation is determined by three factors: the level of risk, the holding time, and the source of rewards.

Understanding Investing

The process of progressively building up one's wealth is called investing. The anticipation of a statistically significant positive return in the form of income or price increase is the basic idea behind investing.

The range of assets in which to invest and generate a return is extremely broad.

RISK MANAGEMENT FOR INVESTMENT

Risk management is a critical technique for making investment decisions. Risk management entails recognizing and analyzing risk in an investment before deciding whether or not to accept it given the expected rewards. Some typical risk metrics include standard deviation, Sharpe ratio, beta, value at risk (VaR), conditional value at risk (CVaR), and R-squared.

Standard deviation is computed by dividing the square root of the sum of squared deviations from an investment's mean by the number of data points in the set.
Semi-deviation is a measurement method that only measures a portion of an investment's risk profile, as opposed to standard deviation.

The semi-deviation is calculated similarly to the standard deviation, but it can be used to focus just on an investment's downside or risk of loss potential because only half of the distribution curve is identified.

Sharpe Ratio
The Sharpe ratio assesses investment performance while accounting for associated risks. To calculate the Sharpe ratio, subtract the risk-free rate of return from the overall projected return of an investment. The remaining return is then split by the connected investment's standard deviation. The end result is a ratio that compares the specific return of an investment to the level of volatility that an investor must assume when keeping the investment. The Sharpe ratio measures whether an investment's return is worth the associated risk.

The Sortino ratio is a version of the Sharpe ratio that eliminates the impacts of upward price movements on standard deviation in order to focus on the distribution of returns that are less than the goal or necessary return. In addition, the Sortino ratio removes the risk-free rate of return from the numerator of the formula.

The Sharpe ratio is particularly effective for comparing different alternatives. This metric enables investors to readily determine which firms or industries offer the highest returns for any given degree of risk.

The Sharpe ratio is computed by deducting the risk-free rate of return from an investment's total return. Then divide the result by the standard deviation of the investment's excess return.

The Treynor Ratio is a version of the Sharpe ratio that compares a portfolio's beta to the rest of the market. The volatility of an investment in relation to the market as a whole is measured by its beta. The Treynor ratio is used to measure if an investor is getting appropriately compensated for assuming more risk than the market. The Treynor ratio is determined by dividing the investment's beta by the portfolio's return minus the risk-free rate.

Beta

Beta is a measure of the systematic risk that an individual asset or sector has in comparison to the overall stock market. The market is usually used as a beta benchmark when comparing investments, and it always has a beta of one.

If a security's beta equals one, it has the same volatility profile as the whole market. A security with a beta greater than one is more volatile than the market. A security is less volatile than the market if its beta value is less than one.

Beta is particularly beneficial when comparing an investment to the broader market.
Beta is computed by dividing the covariance of an investment's excess returns and the variance of excess market returns by the risk-free rate. Beta can also be used to assess a security's level of volatility in comparison to the whole market. For example, say a security's beta is 1.5. The security is deemed 50% more volatile than the market. Beta is useful for comparing securities; at a glance, beta indicates that an investment with a beta of 1.5 is more volatile than one with a beta of 1.3.

Value at Risk (VaR).
Value at Risk (VaR) is a statistical indicator that determines the level of risk associated with a portfolio or organization. The VaR calculates the maximum potential loss with a level of confidence for a given time period. Consider a portfolio of investments with a one-year 10% VaR of $5 million. As a result, the portfolio has a 10% risk of losing $5 million over time. One-year span.

VaR is most useful for determining the likelihood of a specific outcome occurring.
There are several different ways to calculate Value at Risk, each with its own formula:

The simplest method is historical simulation, which uses prior market data over a defined period to apply the results to an investment's current state.

When dealing with larger data sets, the parametric method, also known as the variance-covariance method, comes in handy.

The Monte Carlo method is best suited for the most complex simulations, assuming that the probability of risk for each risk factor is known.

Conditional Value at Risk (CVaR).

Another risk measurement is Conditional Value at Risk (CVaR), which is used to estimate an investment's tail risk. The CVaR, which is an extension of the VaR, analyzes the possibility of a break in the VaR with a particular level of certainty. It aims to determine what happens to investments that exceed their maximum loss thresholds. A measurement that is closer to the tail end of a distribution is more sensitive to occurrences.

CVaR is particularly beneficial for investors seeking to determine the greatest potential loss for situations that are statistically unlikely to occur. For example, suppose a risk manager believes the average loss on an investment is $10 million in the worst-case scenario for a portfolio. As a result, the CVaR, or expected shortfall, is $10 million for this one percent of the investment's distribution curve. The VaR loss for this investment will most certainly be less than $10 million, given the CVaR loss frequently surpasses the distribution boundary of the VaR simulation.

R-squared

R-squared is a statistical measure that calculates the percentage of a fund's or security's movements that can be explained by changes in a benchmark index.

The S&P 500 Index is the benchmark for equities and equity funds.

R-squared values range from zero to one and are generally given as a percentage (0% to 100%). An R-squared value of 0.9 suggests 90% of the analysis accounts for 90% of the variation within the data. Risk models with higher R-squared values suggest that the independent variables being employed inside the model are explaining more of the variation of the dependent variable.
R-Squared is particularly effective when attempting to determine why the price of an investment changes. It's a consequence of a financial model that clarifies what variables impact the outcome of other variables.

The formula to get R-Squared is to divide the unexplained variance (the sum of the squares of residuals) by the total variance (the whole sum of squares). Then, subtract this quotient from 1.
Mutual fund investors are often encouraged to avoid actively managed funds with high R-squared ratios which are generally condemned by analysts as being "closet" index funds. In these instances, with each basket of investments functioning fairly similar to each other, it makes little sense to pay more fees for professional management when you can obtain the same or close results from an index fund.

Categories of Risks
Risk management is classified into two categories: systematic and unsystematic risk. Every investment is subject to both types of risk, however the risk composition varies between assets.

Systematic Risk

There is a systemic risk to the market overall. This risk affects all security and is both unpredictable and uncontrollable. However, systemic risk can be reduced through hedging. Political upheaval, for example, is a systemic risk that can have an impact on entire financial sectors such as bond, stock and currency markets. All stocks in these industries would suffer a detrimental impact.

Unsystematic Risk.

The second type of risk, unsystematic risk, is associated with a specific company or sector. It is also known as diversifiable risk, and it can be minimized by diversifying your assets. This risk is unique to a particular stock or industry, and each security has a different level of unsystematic risk. When an investor buys oil stock, he or she assumes all of the risks involved with the oil business and the company.

To guard against unsystematic risk, the investor may aim to take the opposite side of, or hedge, his position by buying a put option on crude oil or on the firm, or he may look to minimize the risk through diversification by buying stock in an unrelated company or industry. The ultimate goal is to lower the portfolio's overall exposure to the oil industry and the specific company.

Why is Risk Management Important

Risk management in investing is crucial since it assesses the potential upsides and downsides of securities. Instead than focusing simply on an investment's predicted profits, it takes into account the potential loss of cash and warns the investor of any undesirable results.

How Do You Assess the Risk of an Investment?
There are numerous techniques to assess risk. Beta is a risk or volatility metric that compares an investment to the overall market. The standard deviation measures the departure of performance from an investment's average. The Sharpe Ratio determines whether an investment's profits adequately compensate an investor for the level of risk assumed.

What are the two main types of risk?
There are two major categories of risk: systematic risk and unsystematic risk. Systematic risk has an impact on everything. It refers to the overall risk associated with investment. Unsystematic risk is more particular to one company, industry, or area. You are stuck with systematic risk, but you have unlimited flexibility over how much unsystematic risk you want to take.

The Bottom Line
Many investors focus solely on investment profits, with little regard for investment risk. The risk measures examined can help balance the risk-reward equation. The good news for investors is that these indicators can be found on many financial websites and are automatically calculated. These measures are also used in many investment research reports. When evaluating the quality of a stock, bond, or mutual fund investment, volatility risk and risk management should also be considered.

KEY TAKEAWAYS
Risk management is the process of comparing an investment's returns to its risk, with the hope that a higher level of risk will be compensated by a higher predicted return.

Using statistical techniques that have historically predicted investment risk and volatility, risk—or the chance of a loss—can be measured. Standard deviation, Sharpe ratio, and beta are among the most often utilized risk management approaches.

Value at Risk and other variations not only measure the possible cash impact, but also provide a confidence interval for the likelihood of a result. Risk management also manages systematic and unsystematic risk, the two major categories of risk that affect all investments.

Standard Deviation

The standard deviation of data is calculated as the difference between its expected and actual values. The standard deviation is a commonly used metric for calculating an investment's historical volatility in relation to its annual return. It shows how much of the present return deviates from the expected historical normal returns. For example, a stock with a high standard deviation has higher volatility and is hence deemed riskier. Standard deviation is most effective when combined with an investment's average return to assess the dispersion from historical outcomes.

CHAPTER 7

LEVERAGING REAL ESTATE FOR WEALTH

How to Increase Your Real Estate Net Worth With Leveraging

Investing in real estate has become a popular method for diversifying your financial portfolio. Everywhere we look, we are reminded of the advantages of purchasing property, from the numerous infomercials offering real estate seminars to the home programs touting the amazing value of managing or flipping rental homes.

But it isn't so simple. After all, purchasing a rental property is not the same as investing in stocks—you cannot simply throw in a few dollars here and there and become a property owner. You need money to make that purchase. Furthermore, the process might be time-consuming and tedious. Not to mention the risks, particularly if you do not conduct adequate research. But is there a method to enter the market while improving your net worth? Consider leveraging leverage to your advantage. This allows you to put little to no money down and use debt to generate a return.

Ways to Access Leverage
The simplest method to gain leverage is to use your own funds. A normal 20% down payment on a mortgage gives you 100% ownership of the home

you want to live in. Some financing solutions allow you to put even less money down.

If you buy the house as an investment, your partners may contribute some or even all of the funds. Similarly, some sellers may be willing to finance a portion of the purchase price of the property they want to sell. Such an agreement allows you to buy a home with little or no money down.

Example of Leveraging

Consider the typical real estate acquisition requirement of 20% down payment. That is $100,000 for a $500,000 property. By putting down only 20% of the buying price and borrowing the rest, the buyer is essentially using a little portion of their own funds. A lender is thus responsible for the majority of the funding. That is why real estate investors frequently refer to the remaining 80% of the purchase price as someone else's money.

Assume the property appreciates at 5% each year. This means the borrower's net worth will increase to $525,000 in just 12 months. Comparing this gain to the gain from a purchase made wholly, without a loan, demonstrates the usefulness of the leveraging technique. For example, the same borrower may have utilized the $100,000 to pay in full for a $100,000 home.

Assuming the same 5% rate of appreciation, the buyer's net value from the purchase of an all-cash $100,000 property would increase $5,000 over 12 months, compared to $25,000 for the more expensive property. The $20,000 difference indicates the potential net worth growth offered by the utilization of leverage. Consider a 5% annual increase over the course of 20 years. Over time, using leverage can have a big and favorable impact on your net worth.

The Dangers of Leverage

Now, for the terrible news. All of this sounds terrific, but there is a drawback. You can use leverage to your advantage or disadvantage. To demonstrate, consider our previous example. If you utilize a $100,000 down payment to buy a $500,000 property, then real estate prices in your neighborhood fall steadily over several years, leverage works in reverse. If your $500,000 property depreciates by 5% in the first year, it could be worth $475,000 after that. If prices continue to rise, your property could soon be worth $451,250, resulting in a $48,750 loss of equity.

You can use leverage to your advantage or disadvantage.
Under the same 5% price-decline scenario, if $100,000 was spent on an all-cash purchase of a $100,000 property, the buyer would have lost only $5,000 in the first year home values fell—far less than that more expensive home.

In real estate areas where prices have fallen dramatically, homeowners may end up owing more money than the house is worth. For investors, falling prices might reduce or eliminate earnings. If rentals fall, the property may be unable to be rented at a price sufficient to meet the mortgage and other expenditures. If you are thinking about becoming a landlord, there are several considerations to consider.

Cons of Leveraging Multiple Properties

The problems get even more severe when numerous units are involved, as commercial real estate investors frequently put down as little money as possible. The idea is to leverage your money by gaining complete control of the assets while only putting down 20% of the value. Consider the $500,000 in our previous scenario, but now imagine it's a tiny apartment building. Because it was purchased with a $100,000 down payment, if the building's value falls by 30%, the property is only worth $350,000, but the investor is still required to pay interest and principal on the entire $400,000 loan.

If the investor's rent income falls, the property may go into default. If the investor uses the cash flow from that property to pay the mortgage on other properties, the loss of income could have a domino effect, resulting in the entire portfolio going into foreclosure due to one bad loan on one property.

Avoiding Leveraging Risks
Now that you've understood the fundamentals of leverage in real estate, as well as some of the drawbacks, you may believe it's difficult to generate a solid return utilizing this strategy. Don't worry, it's simply a matter of employing common sense. Real estate, like any other type of investment, has risk. Although leverage might be beneficial, there are a few crucial things you should avoid in order to get a competitive advantage.

First, don't predict what will happen before it does. Past performance is not always a reliable predictor of future outcomes, especially in the property market. If you notice that property values in a specific location have risen by 5% to 10% over a given period of time, this does not imply that they will continue on that path.

Next, plan your budget and understand what you're getting yourself into. If you make a smaller down payment, the amount of your loan will increase. This means you'll need to make a bigger mortgage payment. You may have to account for decreased vacancy rates, a harsher economy, and problematic tenants—all of which will be your responsibility. Finally, you are still responsible for the mortgage payment, so you must ensure that you can maintain your financial stability in any situation.

The Bottom Line
Images of such leveraged transactions bring to mind late-night infomercials in which smooth-talking marketers claim that you can make millions of dollars by buying houses with no money down. While it is conceivable, we do not advocate taking this approach.

Fortunately, you don't have to. There are less creative ways to employ leverage, allowing you to acquire real estate with little or no money down. In fact, most people use leverage when they take out a mortgage to buy a property, even if they don't realize it. They repay the loan over years or decades while enjoying the usage of the property. The lesson of the story is that leverage is a frequent and effective tool—when used wisely.

KEY TAKEAWAYS
Leverage is the use of borrowed capital or debt to boost the potential return on a venture.
In real estate, the most frequent approach to leverage your investment is using your own funds or a mortgage.
Leverage works in your favor when real estate values rise, but it can also result in losses if values fall.

To avoid leveraging risks, make prudent investment decisions and account for mortgage payments, vacancies, and a challenging economy.

What is Leverage?

Leverage is the use of various financial instruments or borrowed funds, sometimes known as debt, to boost the potential return on an investment. It is often used on both Wall Street and Main Street to discuss the real estate market. Leverage is a tactic used by both individuals and businesses to increase the possibility for gains while also increasing the risk of failure.

While there is the possibility of a good return (for example, when real estate values rise), utilizing leverage can be a two-edged sword. That's because it might also result in losses if the investment goes in the opposite direction. Real estate price declines result in losses.

SMART PROPERTY INVESTMENT STRATEGIES

Introduction: In an age where financial literacy is critical to ensuring a prosperous future, property investment stands out as a dependable and rewarding option. This chapter attempts to shed light on the strategic aspects of property investment, providing insights for both experienced investors and newcomers looking to enter the real estate market.

Understanding the Basics: Property investment entails more than just purchasing a piece of real estate. It is critical to understand market dynamics, property cycles, and potential return on investment. Conduct extensive study on local real estate trends, anticipated developments, and economic data that may affect property values.

Risk Management: As with any investment, property carries its own set of dangers. A strong risk management strategy is necessary for dealing with everything from market changes to unforeseen maintenance bills. Diversification across different types of properties and geographical locations can help reduce risks while increasing returns.

Financial Planning: Before delving into real estate investment, evaluate your financial situation. Create a detailed budget that includes not only the property purchase but also continuing expenses like property taxes, insurance, and upkeep. Consider talking with a financial professional to ensure that your investment is in line with your overall financial objectives.

Choosing the Right Property: The key to a successful property investment is to select the right asset. Look for assets with high growth potential, close proximity to amenities, and a consistent rental market. Perform due diligence on the property's history, condition, and prospects for future development or improvement.

Leveraging Technology: Utilize technological tools to improve your property investment journey. Leveraging technology can help you maximize your investment approach, from real estate apps that provide market information to property management software that streamlines day-to-day operations.

Extended Goals: Investing in real estate is a journey, not a race. Take a long-term view, acknowledging that property values may fluctuate during shorter time periods. A well-chosen property, along with a careful and deliberate strategy, can generate significant profits over time.

Network and Learn: Connect with other investors, attend industry events, and stay up to current on market developments. Building a network can lead to useful insights and possibilities. Continuous learning is essential in a dynamic market, so consider joining real estate investment forums and seeking mentorship from experienced investors.

Conclusion: When done correctly and strategically, property investing may be a powerful vehicle for wealth creation. Understanding the market, controlling risks, and adopting a long-term perspective can help investors unleash the potential for financial prosperity through real estate. Whether you're an experienced investor or a newbie, the world of property investment offers prospects for growth and success.

CHAPTER 8

Living Rich For A Lifetime

LIFESTYLE DESIGN FOR WEALTH

Lifestyle Design is the capacity to use your existing resources (money and talents) to create the life your Soul craves and desires. Rather than waiting for a random life to grow around you based on chance, lifestyle design is the act of consciously constructing the life you want to live via hard effort, discipline, and vision.

To have the finest life possible, you must first build it. To master the art of lifestyle design, you must stop viewing money solely as a means of purchasing goods. You must consider money as a tool for achieving the life experiences and freedoms that will make you feel fulfilled, accomplished, and joyful. This is the magic I refer to as "Lifestyle Design." If you can build your future so that you feel good all the time, you will naturally begin to live a life in which you feel good all of the time. In short, choose the things that make you happy, and then use your money to plan your life so that you can experience them as much as possible.

In my perspective, four essential tools are required to master the power of lifestyle design. Here they are:

THE FOUR TOOLS REQUIRED TO DESIGN YOUR LIFE:

#1 SELF-AWARENESS: You won't know what kind of life you want to live unless you can learn to hear yourself think. You must be able to go deep within yourself to discover the source of your own thinking. You must first understand yourself before you can determine what you are supposed to do.

#2: MONEY: A human cannot move mountains in life unless they have the necessary tools and teams. Money is the only resource that can be converted into anything you need. Money can help you purchase the necessary tools and teams to help you achieve your goals.

#3: PSYCHOLOGY: A person cannot enjoy their life unless they convince themselves to be grateful and appreciate what they have. To find happiness, you must first understand your own psyche.
You must also learn how to push yourself past your fears and sorrow in order to see and construct the life that amazing people live. You must think you can do it, and then persuade yourself that you are intended to do it, no matter how frightening or difficult the trip to your goals may be.

#4: SPIRITUALITY: Why are you alive? What were you designed to do? What does your spirit want to see, experience, and create during your lifetime? Before you can design a strategy for what, where, and how, you must first determine why. Spirituality can help you discover your why.

LIFESTYLE DESIGN EXPLORED:

Let's break down these four individual concepts (Awareness, Money, Psychology, and Spirituality) so you can see how, when combined, they can help you create the life you've always wanted.

LIFESTYLE DESIGN TOOL #1: SELF-AWARENESS.
First of all, who are you? Answer that question now. If you cannot answer the question, "Who are you?"" with a confident statement consisting of a few powerful and meaningful lines outlining your reasoning, motives, and ambitions, then I recommend that you start by becoming aware of who you are.

How do you do it? Turn off the television. Close your social media accounts. Abandon friends that blind you to reality. Abandon any influence in your life that is causing you to think things that are not your own, and go out on a journey to discover which of your thoughts are your own.

Find your own peaceful spot of stillness where you can learn to listen to the thoughts that arise from your spirit. Personally, I do this by taking long walks, sometimes accompanied by music or podcasts with a positive and illuminating message, and simply becoming comfortable with the thoughts in my head. I meet, appraise, and examine them. I question myself, "Where do my thoughts come from?" What are they instructing me to do? What is the basic aim of these?"

I analyze whether my thoughts are coming from a place of insecurity or confidence. If my thoughts are driven by insecurity, causing me to overcompensate for my natural actions, I attempt to discover confidence in who I truly am. If my thoughts come from a place of confidence, I do everything I can to encourage them to grow because they are the ones that will lead me to develop into the person I was meant to be.

But, before I try to build my life around the voice of my thoughts, I spend 80% of my time figuring out who I am. Achieving actual life goals only provides 20% of happiness. The remaining 80% of happiness stems from the time and work required to shine a light into the darkest depths of your soul and discover why you must achieve this objective in order to be happy. The first tool for mastering lifestyle design is to unflinchingly stare into the depths of your soul and become profoundly aware of who you are and what you are supposed to do with your life.

Lifestyle Design Tool #2: Money
How do you see money? Do you see money as a method to get additional goods that you don't need? Or do you see money as a means of achieving complete control over your time, allowing you to create a life that allows you to live the life you were born to live?

If you see money as a means to get more things, you will always be trapped in a lifestyle that is dependent on a job-like existence to earn more money to purchase more things. The need for more money and more goods will never go away if that is what you live for, which means you will never be able to leave your job to earn the money to acquire them.

However, if you see money as a means of achieving complete freedom over your time, you will begin to utilize it to develop a life in which you are free to think and create as you like. The most important thing affluent people utilize to construct their dream life is time to allow themselves to learn, progress, and eventually succeed. DON'T regard money as a means to purchase additional items. Consider money to be a means of gaining complete control over your time, allowing you to become a wiser, more skillful human person, and wealth will frequently result as a byproduct of being a more gifted human.

Lifestyle Design Tool #3: Psychology:
Abandon the pessimistic mindset. Accept the optimistic mindset. Trick your mind into seeing the good in everything. You will never be happy unless you learn to appreciate your existing fortunes.

Forgive more. Share without expecting more. Please help more. When you choose to participate in healthy activities, you will feel more pleased of yourself.

Wealth is an act of purposefully feeling better about yourself, and doing the things that will make you feel better about yourself. When you feel good about yourself and have a financial cushion to shield yourself from the harsh realities of running out of resources, you can begin to enjoy life.

Lifestyle Design Tool #4: Spirituality
The world is very huge and strong. It is much larger than the finite number of brain cells in your own mind. Use the vastness of the planet and the spiritual energies that exist to discover greater visions than you could have imagined on your own.

I believe in God. I intentionally use my faith in God to create concepts and visions that I would not be able to imagine if I didn't believe in a higher purpose for my existence.

If you have had a horrible experience with man-made religion, I am sad and have a lot of empathy for you. However, do not allow their faults limit the potential of your life and your relationship with God.

Use the power of spirituality to gain the courage to look beyond your own selfish needs and live for the greater good of assisting, sharing, and inspiring. Jesus' teachings are my personal inspiration for living my life. Having a broader, deeper calling than just working, buying, and dying has allowed me to construct my life in ways I could not have done on my own.

CONCLUSION

"Lifestyle Design" refers to the capacity to combine the skills of self-awareness, finance, psychology, and spirituality to design the life that brings you the most happiness. I recently saw a quote that summed up the subject. The phrase stated, "Build icebergs with your life, not skyscrapers." This concept struck a chord with me because it reminded me that life's accomplishments (skyscrapers) are visible to everybody. However, it is the icebergs in life (the force of the spirit and subconscious) that guide people to live their full potential. The icebergs, or Lifestyle Design tools, are where all of the greatest quests and lives begin.

CREATING A BALANCED AND FULFILLING LIFE

You go to work and want to give it your all, even if it means working a few additional hours. However, you still want to spend time with your family and friends. And after weeks or even months of attempting to accomplish the
impossible aim of giving your all in both areas, you find that it is harmful to your entire well-being.

We get it. It is stressful.

In today's fast-paced and demanding environment, striking a work-life balance has become increasingly difficult. The demands of job deadlines, obligations, and the drive to excel frequently consume our personal time and well-being.
However, attaining work-life balance is not only crucial for our health and happiness but also for our long-term success. Today, we'll look at the significance of striking a healthy balance between work and life, as well as some practical ideas to help you do so.

Why is work-life balance important?
Research regularly reveals that having a healthy work-life balance has both rewards and disadvantages.

A healthy balance not only improves our overall well-being, but it also boosts job happiness, productivity, and psychological health. Companies that prioritize work-life balance are two times more productive than those that do not.

So, how can we accomplish this?

You can begin implementing numerous changes in your life that will make a significant effect.

Achieving Work-Life Balance
- Begin setting boundaries (yes, even for yourself).

According to 32.8% of polled workers, personal perfectionism is the most significant hindrance to achieving a healthy work-life balance. While managers play an important role in trespassing limits, we must keep ourselves accountable when it comes to saying "no" to specific responsibilities.

Defining Boundaries: Boundaries are the standards and boundaries we establish for ourselves in order to maintain our emotional, physical, and mental health. They provide a framework for protecting our personal space, values, and individuality while also allowing us to connect with others in a way that is respectful and understandable.

Types of Boundaries and Examples:

Physical boundaries refer to our personal space and physical well-being. Setting physical boundaries could entail expressing preferences for intimate touch or limiting how close people can go to us physically.

Emotional boundaries are about safeguarding and managing our emotional well-being. Examples include expressing our emotions and wants openly and selecting how much personal information we are willing to share with others.

Intellectual limits refer to our thoughts, beliefs, and opinions. Setting intellectual boundaries entails having respectful talks, being open to new ideas, and limiting fruitless or unpleasant debates.

Time boundaries entail putting restrictions on how we use our time and energy. Time boundaries include saying "no" to excessive commitments, prioritizing self-care, and maintaining a good work-life balance.

Material limits refer to our things, finances, and personal space. Examples include establishing standards for borrowing or lending objects, safeguarding personal belongings, and defining financial limitations and expectations.

Real-life Examples: To demonstrate these types of boundaries, consider scenarios like politely asking a friend to respect your personal space when they invade it without consent (physical boundary), expressing to a family member how their hurtful comments impact you and setting expectations for respectful communication (emotional boundary), redirecting a heated and disrespectful debate towards a more constructive tone or choosing to disengage (intellectual boundary), and

Setting boundaries is a powerful act of self-care and self-respect. Establishing and maintaining appropriate boundaries allows for personal growth, protects our well-being, and fosters rewarding relationships. So, let us embrace the power of boundaries as we strive for a more balanced and satisfying existence.

Setting limits is a skill that few people master, and while saying "no" may be uncomfortable at first, it is essential if you want to achieve balance.

It is all about practice. It gets easier the more you practice! However, understand that knowing how to set limits in a courteous manner is just as important as knowing when to set them.

- Time Management is Your Best Friend.

Improving productivity and time management skills can greatly help you achieve work-life balance. Time blocking, or setting certain time intervals for different tasks, can help you stay focused and organized.

Prioritizing tasks according to urgency and importance helps you manage your workload more successfully. Learning to delegate jobs to coworkers or

outsource specific activities can help relieve stress and free up time for personal pursuits. This may be problematic for those who struggle with "personal perfection" as indicated above. However, learning to delegate responsibilities can help you achieve a better work-life balance and develop a team culture that will benefit you and your coworkers in the long run.

"Our approach to productivity isn't just a personal challenge, but a shared contribution to the bigger picture.

- Promoting Wellness and Self-Care

While establishing work-life balance can be an act of self-love in and of itself, giving yourself some "me time" at some point in your day can help you "re-fuel" for the next day.

It might be as simple as listening to music while cooking your favorite cuisine or calling a buddy to catch up. The trick is to make time for activities that make you happy and relaxed.

Incorporating activities such as regular exercise, good food, and adequate sleep into your routine will significantly improve your overall well-being. "I think a lot of people struggle to be motivated by you know, healthiness. And I actually think that if you can put it in perspective, taking downtime can improve your productivity overall and your efficiency when you are working.

- Know When to Ask for Help

Maintaining work-life balance requires developing and sustaining supportive relationships both at work and at home. Effective communication with coworkers, employers, and loved ones can help establish realistic expectations and boundaries.

Whether it's seeking advice from a mentor, sharing workload concerns with your boss, or relying on family and friends for emotional support, developing strong relationships and requesting help when needed can help relieve stress and create a more balanced lifestyle.

"The best thing you can do to catalyze your career is prioritizing your health. Sometimes, we are inclined to think that working longer hours while sacrificing our hobbies, time for family and friends, or a healthy sleep and eating schedule will help us advance in our careers. We tell ourselves that next week will be better if we just get that one more item done. But based on my own experience, this could not be further from the truth. Sure, putting in those extra hours

Achieving work-life balance is an ongoing process that needs conscious effort and self-reflection. Understanding the significance of work-life balance, creating boundaries, increasing productivity, nurturing well-being, and cultivating supportive connections will help you live a peaceful and rewarding life.

Remember that work-life balance is different for everyone, and it is critical to create a balance that corresponds with your unique goals!

THE ROLE OF HEALTH AND WELLNESS IN WEALTH

It's a frequent story: an employee becomes ill, triggering unanticipated medical expenditures. To afford the cost, people withdraw funds from their 401(k) or go into debt. They now worry about money in addition to their health. The accompanying emotional and physical worry has an impact on their work performance and how they present themselves to clients and colleagues.

Physical, emotional, and financial wellbeing are inextricably linked. When we have good physical health, we feel more in control of our lives. This positive mindset encourages us to practice healthy habits such as frequent exercise, healthy eatiing, and sound financial decisions. This promotes general well-being and lowers the risk of diabetes, hypertension, heart disease, and other chronic illnesses.

Poor physical health, on the other hand, frequently leads to despair and anxiety, which in turn produce other health problems such as gastrointestinal disorders, sleeplessness, obesity, and a compromised immune system. There is also an increased risk of alcoholism, drug misuse, and emotional overspending.

So, how can businesses encourage employees to take use of perks that will improve their overall health, financial wellness, and well-being? Personalization holds the key.
When employees are faced with difficult medical issues, personalized, high-touch help can make a big difference.

The Power of Personalization

Employees rarely consider their plan alternatives, except during open enrollment or when confronted with a physical or financial health issue. When employees do participate, they may have to navigate 30 (or more) programs, platforms, or systems. The majority of people lack the time, patience, and insights to assess which solutions are best for the following year, let alone during a crisis.

Technology advancements have enabled employers to assist each employee in making proactive and confident health and wealth decisions in all scenarios, whether managing a crisis or recovering from one. Similar to how Spotify suggests music based on a user's listening history, artificial intelligence (AI) utilizes health and financial data to predict an employee's health, wealth, and well-being needs and make personalized recommendations.

Technology plays an important role in providing focused and timely information. When employees face unpleasant medical issues, individualized, high-touch assistance can go a long way.

The correlation between physical, emotional, and financial well-being is considerable. People prosper when they are confident in their own well-being, both at work and at home. Employers may empower their employees to make confident decisions that improve their well-being and allow them to live their best lives by providing individualized assistance and tools.

How health, wealth, and success are interconnected.

The link between health, wealth, and prosperity is deeper than you may realize. Connecting health and success increases the chances of financial security. Evidence suggests that the relationship between financial wellbeing and health is significant, with enhanced financial security being connected to better physical and mental health outcomes as well as a higher quality of life.

Having more money provides more than just financial security; it can also improve your health. Research indicates that good health, money, and success are inextricably linked. In general, wealth is synonymous with health, indicating a close link between the two. This relationship has little to do with the ability to afford better healthcare. Financial security may improve your mental health and well-being. That's another reason why taking control of your financial destiny is critical.

The Relationship between Health and Wealth
According to research, good health is not only a benefit of money; it can also be a factor in wealth creation. How to Improve Your Health and Wealth Connection
Making beneficial adjustments, whether general life-style improvements or financial habits, is critical to the overall relationship between health, wealth, and prosperity. These modifications and new goals provide you with something worthwhile to work for, and you might begin to feel more fit as you notice gradual progress. Prosperity and health begin with developing better habits such as:

- Cooking healthier meals at home.
- Using your bike to perform quick errands around town instead of driving
- Create a financial vision board with goals to work towards.
- Learning to Budget Effectively
- Meditating every day.

Check your account transactions every night.

There is no guarantee that waking up early, eating well, and having a good night's sleep will make you wealthy. However, research shows that it does put you on the correct course toward success.

CHAPTER 9

PASSING DOWN WEALTH TO FUTURE GENERATIONS

Assets inherited from one generation to the next are referred to as generational wealth.
Creating generational wealth can give long-term financial security and possibilities for your children, grandkids, and others.

Learn why generational wealth is vital, how to create the groundwork for your family's wealth, and how to ensure that your legacy is passed down as efficiently as possible.

Challenges of Creating Generational Wealth
Building generational wealth is a difficult task, especially if you grow up in poverty or encounter structural impediments. Unfortunately, this has been the case for many oppressed groups in this country.

If you want to develop generational wealth, you can make a few financial actions that can help you get there.

- Create a strong financial foundation.

Building generational wealth requires both great leadership and sound financial judgments. You may teach your family the fundamentals of healthy personal finance, including the excellent practices listed below.

- Prioritize savings.

Many people get into the trap of promising to save what's left over at the end of the month but never following through, or they spend over their means. A better strategy is to design a budget to manage your spending so that you always have funds available to save, and then set up an automatic monthly payment to yourself.

Here is how to start:
Choose a percentage or dollar amount that you can devote to savings goals once your expenses are addressed.
If you have multiple savings goals, create different accounts for each.
Consider opening a high-yield savings account that earns interest on top of your contributions.
Set up automatic deposits into each savings account and watch them grow.

For longer-term savings goals, consider investing in certificate of deposit (CD) accounts, which provide a guaranteed return.

Build an emergency fund.
One of the most significant instruments for accumulating generational wealth is to ensure financial security in the event of an emergency or loss of income. Here's when having an emergency fund comes in.

Often, not having an emergency fund pushes people into debt or causes them to cash out retirement savings, which not only incurs penalties but also has a significant opportunity cost.

Finally, you want to have enough money saved to cover a few months' worth of costs, which will take some time to accumulate. In the meantime, focus on making regular, automated contributions and saving more aggressively if you identify methods to cut costs or generate new revenue streams. Most importantly, avoid the temptation to remove money from the account; it should only be used in actual situations.

Involve kids in money conversations.
One often-overlooked facet of establishing a solid financial foundation is incorporating your family, particularly your children, in the discussion. This way, they can learn financial principles from a young age with you.

Invest in education.
Once you've made some headway with your emergency fund, you can devote part of your discretionary cash to other major financial goals. A popular option is to save for your children's education. If you want to develop generational wealth, consider college savings for your children as an investment in their future earning potential.

Of course, the expenses of education continue to grow, and it may not be the best option for all. Before investing in education, you should first assess your financial status and life aspirations.
Consider starting a 529 plan, which is a tax-free account that may be utilized for qualified school costs.

Invest in the financial markets.
The sooner you start, the better your chances of creating meaningful money. "The strength of compound interest means that small initial

investments made regularly over time can add up to a sizable sum thanks to early initiation.

While investing in the stock market carries some risk, diversifying your investments across stocks, bonds, and other assets allows you to balance risk with growth potential. One popular technique for beginners is to invest in index funds, which are collections of stocks designed to replicate the performance of key market indexes such as the S&P 500.

The secret to investing in the stock market is to think long term, riding out downturns because it usually recovers.

Invest in real estate.
Real estate is another popular investment option, due to the possibility for rental income and property value appreciation. Furthermore, it is a significant investment to pass on to your next of kin.
"Investigating several kinds of properties, such as commercial and residential, may help you diversify your real estate portfolio.

If you aren't ready for that kind of investment or don't want the responsibility of managing a property, I recommend looking into real estate investment trusts.

Create and preserve assets.
Building money is only the first step toward creating generational wealth. The next step is to secure your assets so that they can be passed on to future generations. You also want your heirs to be able to keep as much of their inheritance (if applicable), which is where tax considerations come into play.

Consider the following activities to safeguard your children's safety and financial stability.

Create an Estate Plan.
As your assets expand and become more complex, collaborating with financial advisers and attorneys on estate planning is the wise decision. Some considerations are:

Establishing a business that is heirloomable
Consider life insurance. "One of the most tax-effective methods to transfer money is through life insurance.
Ensuring that additional insurance needs are addressed. Make sure you're insured in the event of a catastrophic occurrence concerning your home, car, or medical situation. If not, a single incident or lawsuit might deplete your savings.

Maximize Tax Benefits.
A variety of tax-efficient investment techniques and vehicles can help you keep a larger portion of your profits. Several strategies include:

Tax-deferred accounts include traditional individual retirement accounts (IRAs) and 401(k) plans, which provide an upfront tax advantage as you invest. When you remove money from your retirement account, you must pay taxes.
Roth IRAs and Roth 401(k)s are tax-exempt when withdrawn since contributions are made after taxes.

Health Savings Accounts (HSAs) allow you to contribute tax-free and get tax-free growth. Then, if utilized for qualified medical expenses, the money is also tax-free.

Work with a tax accountant or financial counselor to determine which techniques are best for you and, ultimately, to save as much money as possible from taxes.

Avoid Debt and Financial Pitfalls.
Living within your means and maintaining a strong emergency fund are the two most effective methods to prevent unnecessary, high-interest debt, such as huge credit card balances. These forms of borrowing expenses can impede you from progressing toward your savings and wealth-building goals.

If you do have debt, pay off the highest-interest accounts first, while continuing to contribute to your emergency fund and retirement accounts. When opportunities arise, try to use any financial windfalls, such as tax returns or monetary gifts, to pay off significant sums.

How to pass down generational wealth.
The final part of generational wealth is ensuring that it ends up where you want it to. This includes having your wishes legally documented. At the most basic level, you can begin with a will. However, when finances become more sophisticated, you will want to go beyond that.

Setting up a trust is recommended. "A trust can be efficient for bypassing probate if it's set up properly". "And it is private. "It is not a public record if it is held in a trust.

Once you've organized your affairs, keep communication open with your family, informing them of your plans and how to access your paperwork. This is useful in the event of an unexpected emergency in which your family must take over financial responsibilities.

How Can I Begin Building Generational Wealth With Limited Financial Resources?
Take one baby step at a time. Create a budget that allows you to set aside money for savings every month. Make lifestyle choices that will support your financial goals. Also, start saving for retirement as soon as possible so that it has time to grow.

What are some tax-efficient strategies for increasing generational wealth?
There are several tax-efficient options that you may consider adopting, including investing in tax-deferred accounts or Health Savings Accounts. The path you take will be determined by your unique financial situation, so you may want to consult with a tax professional or financial advisor. Furthermore, these professionals can assist you in staying up to date on any new tax requirements that are implemented.

How Can I Protect My Assets and Pass Them Down to Future Generations?
The two most effective strategies to protect your assets are to ensure you are adequately insured (via home, vehicle, and life insurance) and to consult with an estate planner. In addition, make sure you have a will and consider forming a trust.

The Bottom Line

If you're a first-generation wealth builder, committing to the early steps of saving money, creating an emergency fund, and beginning to invest for the long term, as well as sticking to them consistently, will eventually pay off.

Building generational wealth may require some upfront sacrifice, but the short- and long-term benefits make it worthwhile. Throughout your life, you will have the piece of mind that comes from knowing that your loved ones are financially secure. You can also share your expertise and insights with your children and grandchildren to develop solid financial habits in them, allowing them to carry on the family tradition for future generations.

KEY TAKEAWAYS

The term "generational wealth" refers to the transfer of assets from one generation to the next.

Before you can generate generational wealth, you should establish a solid financial foundation by prioritizing savings, building an emergency fund, and planning for the future.

Generational wealth can give long-term financial security while also creating opportunity for your children and future generations.

Investing in education, financial markets, and real estate, as well as developing and maintaining assets, are examples of generational wealth creation strategies.

Maximizing tax breaks and minimizing debt are critical for accumulating generational wealth.

Importance of Creating Generational Wealth

Achieving financial success involves a lot of effort, sacrifice, and forethought. Not only may it help you enjoy things during your lifetime, but it can also help your descendants realize the advantages of your legacy and live a financially comfortable existence when you pass away.

Think of it as a wealth snowball. For example, generational wealth sets the path for better educational options and, as a result, higher earning potential for your children. Then they can continue to build on that foundation for their children (your grandchildren).

ESTATE PLANNING AND LEGACY BUILDING

Estate planning is an important step in ensuring your family's future and leaving a lasting legacy. It entails making smart decisions about how your assets and properties will be handled and dispersed after your death.

While this may not be the most pleasant topic to discuss, good estate planning guarantees that your loved ones are cared for and that your desires are followed. In this chapter, we'll look at the importance of estate planning and the numerous benefits it provides to you and your family.

What is Estate Planning?

Estate planning is the act of structuring, administering, and dispersing your assets in accordance with your intentions while also ensuring your loved ones' financial well-being. The key goals are to reduce taxes, ensure assets are dispersed efficiently, and provide for your family's future. To successfully manage and transfer assets, estate planners frequently create a living trust or revocable trust.

Why Is Estate Planning Important?

A multitude of factors make estate planning important. It gives you peace of mind knowing that your loved ones will be taken care of. It also helps to minimize family conflicts and legal issues that can occur without a clear plan in place. Furthermore, it enables you to leave a legacy that represents your beliefs and priorities.

Benefits of Estate Planning.

Wealth Preservation and Asset Distribution
Estate planning is a critical component of comprehensive wealth management, ensuring the preservation of your hard-earned money. With family financial planning, you can designate how your assets should be transferred to your beneficiaries using legal procedures such as wills and trusts. This approach helps to prevent lengthy and costly probate proceedings, resulting in a smoother succession of your estate.

Minimizing Tax Burden
One of the most significant advantages of estate planning is the possibility to reduce the tax burden on your estate. Estate taxes can be reduced through a variety of options, including gifting, family limited partnerships, and qualified personal residence trusts. Effective tax planning is an important aspect of estate planning because it allows you to leave more of your assets to your loved ones rather than the tax authorities.

Protecting Beneficiaries
Estate planning ensures that your property is distributed to the appropriate recipients. By expressing your preferences in legal documents, you can protect your loved ones' financial interests and provide them with a stable and secure future. Establishing a trust protects your beneficiary's financial interests.

Charitable Giving and Philanthropy
Estate planning is essential for those who are committed to giving back to their community or supporting charity causes. Tools such as charitable

remainder trusts and donor-advised funds enable you to leave a lasting legacy for the causes that are most important to you.

Making Decisions Easy

Estate preparation often includes essential healthcare considerations, such as drafting a living will outlining your medical treatment wishes. Healthcare directives and healthcare powers of attorney appoint someone to make medical choices on your behalf if you are unable to do so. This guarantees that your wishes for medical treatment are fulfilled, giving you peace of mind.

Key Takeaways

Estate planning is an important step in ensuring your family's future and leaving a lasting legacy that represents your values. Estate planning has numerous benefits, including wealth preservation, tax minimization, beneficiary protection, charitable giving, and healthcare decision-making. To begin the estate planning process, consider following actionable steps:

Consult an estate planning attorney to develop a complete plan.
Take inventory of your assets and properties.
Ensure that the people you care about understand your wishes
Regularly examine and revise your estate plan as circumstances change.
By taking these measures, you can protect your family's heritage and ensure that your wishes are carried out for future generations. Consider working with a qualified financial expert to help you with your estate planning.

CHAPTER 10

Mastering the Art of Giving Back

PHILANTHROPY AND SOCIAL IMPACT

Philanthropy is becoming an increasingly important and revolutionary component of wealth management. Wealthy and influential people have long been associated with philanthropic activities. Individuals and organizations, on the other hand, are increasingly incorporating values and societal contributions into their wealth management processes, rather than simply accomplishing financial goals.

Thus, the function of philanthropy in wealth management is becoming increasingly important, where many wealthy individuals and families are allocating their wealth to social causes.

Benefits of Philanthropy for Wealth Management
The importance of philanthropy in wealth management goes beyond the act of giving.

Purpose-driven investment: Philanthropy enables people and organizations to match their wealth with their values and social goals. Philanthropy becomes an extension of one's life purpose when it is used to support causes that align with personal ideals.

Tax breaks are frequently available for charitable donations. Individuals can reduce their tax liability while also making a good contribution to society by carefully donating to charitable organizations.

Reputation enhancement: Philanthropic actions frequently result in improved personal or company reputations. A conscious giving plan can become an important part of personal branding, distinguishing you as someone who values more than just financial achievement.

Corporate Social Responsibility (CSR) alignment: Businesses can combine philanthropy with Corporate Social Responsibility (CSR) programs. This helps to meet statutory duties while also helping to brand development. An effective CSR plan can improve customer loyalty, employee involvement, and the overall firm image.

Individuals and businesses can help to create long-term change through philanthropy. Wealth's impact extends beyond momentary alleviation by supporting education, healthcare, the environment, and other sustainable efforts, resulting in long-term community empowerment.

Networking opportunities: Philanthropic initiatives might lead to new connections and collaborations. Participating in nonprofit boards, events, or collaborations can lead to networking with like-minded people and groups. These partnerships can help people achieve their personal and professional goals while also strengthening the humanitarian mission.

Improving investment methods: Combining philanthropy with investment strategies results in a broader perspective on wealth management. Ethical investments, ESG (Environmental, Social, Governance) criteria, and impact investing become inextricably linked with philanthropic objectives, paving the road for a more sustainable future.

The benefits of generosity in wealth management go beyond the monetary component. Where the economic environment is broad and social causes abound, charity adds meaning and compassion to the journey of wealth creation.

Strategies for Effective Philanthropy.
For philanthropy to be genuinely meaningful, it must be carried out wisely and strategically. Here are some ideas for successful generosity in wealth management:

Identify clear objectives: Determine what you hope to accomplish through donation. Are you committed to education, healthcare, poverty eradication, or other social causes? Clear objectives direct effective philanthropic initiatives and prevent disorganized or ineffectual attempts.

Choose the correct vehicles: There are several instruments available for philanthropic giving, including establishing a foundation, contributing to existing NGOs, and impact investment. It is critical to conduct research and analysis on these possibilities in order to choose the one that best fits your goals, interests, and financial plans.

Consult experts: Work with professionals who are familiar with the legal, tax, and societal elements of charity. Their knowledge can help you navigate complex regulatory landscapes, ensuring that your philanthropic initiatives are effective, compliant, and meaningful.

Measure impact: Effective giving necessitates monitoring and assessing impact. Regular assessments, such as reports, field visits, or third-party evaluations, can provide insight into how your contributions are actually making an impact. It fosters transparency and accountability, allowing for required changes and enhancements.

Collaborate and leverage resources: Working with other donors, non-governmental organizations (NGOs), or corporate partners can increase the impact. Pooling resources, knowledge, and efforts can result in more substantive and long-lasting reforms.

Align with SDGs: By adhering to global standards such as the United Nations' Sustainable Development Goals (SDGs), philanthropic operations can be guided more clearly. It provides a globally recognized method to addressing large-scale concerns such as poverty eradication and environmental sustainability.

Incorporate technology: Using technology in charity can increase efficiency and transparency. Platforms that provide real-time tracking, digital donations, and impact reporting make the process more transparent and responsible.

Educate yourself: It is critical to stay informed and up to speed on the sectors in which you invest. Understand the issues, trends, and breakthroughs in the fields you want to help. Participate in discussions, workshops, and conferences to gather insights and tailor your approach accordingly.

Focus on ethical considerations: Make sure that your charity actions are consistent with ethical principles and societal norms. Make informed and responsible decisions by taking into account the long-term repercussions, any unexpected consequences, and cultural sensitivity.

A holistic strategy to charity may ensure that wealth is not just protected and increased, but also used to create a beneficial, long-term impact. Whether you are new to philanthropy or want to improve your current efforts, these techniques provide a road map for properly giving back to society.

Conclusion
The role of charity in wealth management is more than a passing fad; it reflects a more compassionate and socially responsible approach to wealth generation. In India, where social inequities coexist with enormous wealth, philanthropy can play an important role in closing gaps and contributing to overall well-being. Individuals and corporations can make their wealth more meaningful and purposeful by recognizing the role of charity in wealth management and implementing successful philanthropy practices.

BUILDING A WEALTHY COMMUNITY

For many people, reaching financial success may seem like an unachievable goal. However, with the correct advice and resources, wealth accumulation is not only achievable, but also rewarding.

The Importance of Community in Building Wealth

Community is critical to wealth creation and financial success. Individual accomplishment is typically praised in today's society, but the reality is that no one reaches greatness only by their efforts. We are shaped and impacted by the communities in which we live, and having a great community can make a significant difference in wealth creation.

Access to resources and knowledge is one of the primary benefits of community membership. Communities allow people to share their experiences, thoughts, and financial success strategies. Individuals who participate in a wealth-building group can learn from those who have previously achieved their goals, gaining useful insights and avoiding common traps.

A supportive community can also help to motivate and hold people accountable. Surrounding oneself with like-minded people who are also working for financial success fosters an environment of support and motivation. When faced with hardships or losses, the support of a community can be a motivating factor to persevere and stay on course to developing wealth. In addition to practical benefits, the community encourages collaboration and networking.

Building wealth frequently necessitates relationships and connections, and being a member of a community can lead to beneficial collaborations and entrepreneurial chances. Individuals can broaden their professional network and access a plethora of options by attending networking events, seminars, and online forums.

Community fosters a sense of belonging and purpose. Building wealth is more than just saving money; it is also about living a satisfying and meaningful life. Being part of a group that shares your beliefs and aspirations can give you a sense of belonging and purpose, which improves your general well-being and contentment.

How Community Support Can Help You Achieve Your Financial Goals
The influence of community support is an important factor to consider when pursuing financial success.

I realized early on that surrounding myself with like-minded people who have similar goals and desires was critical to my success. He actively pursued networking opportunities in his sector, attending conferences, seminars, and local meetings to interact with other investors and experts. Through these conversations, I developed valuable ties and a solid support network. This community's knowledge sharing, encouragement, and accountability helped him on his path to financial success.

I was able to leverage the experiences and knowledge of others, learning from their successes and failures and thereby accelerate his own advancement. Furthermore, I recognized the value of collaboration. Richard constantly sought up collaborations and joint ventures with people who might complement his abilities and provide distinct viewpoints. They were able to take on larger and more lucrative initiatives by combining resources, sharing risks, and leveraging one other's networks, resulting in a collective wealth increase.

Furthermore, Richard understood the value of giving back to the community that had helped him. He regularly participated in mentorship programs, imparting his skills and experiences to prospective entrepreneurs and investors. By cultivating a culture of collaboration and support, he generated a ripple effect that empowered people to achieve their own financial goals while also enhancing the community as a whole. My journey to financial success exemplifies the strength of community support.

By surrounding himself with like-minded people, engaging with key partners, and aggressively giving back, he not only met his own goals but also helped others succeed. It serves as a reminder that wealth creation is a collaborative effort, and the power of a strong and supportive community should never be underestimated.

The Power of Networking and Collaboration
Networking and teamwork are key instruments that can help you achieve financial success. In today's interconnected world, creating wealth is a collaborative effort that lives on the strength of community. When you surround yourself with others who have similar aims and desires, you gain access to a multitude of knowledge, resources, and opportunities.

Networking helps you to access a wide range of experiences, ideas, and knowledge, broadening your horizons and opening doors you never imagined imaginable. Richard has used networking events, mastermind groups, and partnerships to tap into his peers' aggregate expertise, learning from their successes and disappointments.

By surrounding himself with people that share his passion for wealth creation, Richard has been able to expedite his journey and produce exceptional results. But networking isn't just about what you can get; it's also about what you can give. Collaboration is essential in the process of creating wealth within a community.

By actively participating in collaborative projects, joint ventures, and partnerships, you may pool your skills, resources, and networks to achieve mutually beneficial results. Collaboration allows you to pool your resources to pursue larger investment possibilities, share risks, and maximize rewards. Working together to pursue a common objective can yield significantly higher outcomes than working alone.

Networking and collaboration are not optional steps on the path to financial success; they are necessary ingredients for creating wealth through community. By embracing the power of connections and collaborating with others, you may open up a world of possibilities and pave your way to financial prosperity.

Creating a Robust Support Network for Financial Achievement.
Building a strong support system is critical for financial success. It is commonly said that you are the average of the five people with whom you spend the most time, and this principle also applies to wealth-building. Connecting with like-minded people who share your objectives and aspirations is one of the most effective ways to build a support network.

Surrounding oneself with people who are committed to financial progress and have a good outlook may be extremely motivational and inspiring.

In these groups, you'll discover people eager to share their expertise, experiences, and even resources to assist you on your path to financial success. They can provide advice, important insights, and perhaps lead to new chances that you would not have discovered otherwise. Furthermore, being a part of a supportive group allows you to learn from other people's accomplishments and disappointments. You can learn about alternative financial methods, find new ways to make passive income, and acquire confidence in your abilities.

A robust support system provides you with vital knowledge and resources, as well as inspiration and accountability. When confronted with obstacles or failures, having a network of people who understand your goals and can offer support and encouragement can make all the difference in staying focused and motivated. Building a strong support system requires time and work, but the advantages are immense. By surrounding yourself with people who share your vision for financial success, you'll be on track to reach your goals faster than you ever imagined.

The Role of Education and Continuous Learning in Creating Wealth

Education and continual learning are critical for wealth creation and financial success. It is frequently said that knowledge is power, and this is especially true in the realm of wealth generation. In today's fast changing world, keeping up with the latest trends, strategies, and insights is critical. Investing in your education provides you with the tools and information required to handle the intricacies of the financial landscape.

Richard highlights the value of continuous learning. He believes that education serves as the cornerstone for financial success. I am a witness to the importance of education, since I have relentlessly pursued information throughout my career, continually increasing my skill set and remaining ahead of the curve. One of the primary advantages of continual learning is that it allows you to adjust to changing market conditions.

Economic landscapes change, and what worked yesterday may not work today. By being informed and constantly updating your knowledge, you can uncover fresh possibilities, manage risks, and make informed decisions that will propel you to financial success. Furthermore, education exposes you to a diverse set of viewpoints and tactics. It enables you to learn from the achievements and failures of others, providing useful insights that you can apply to your own wealth-building efforts.

By researching diverse investing techniques, financial instruments, and company concepts, you may create a well-rounded approach to wealth growth. In addition to formal schooling, developing a constant learning mentality is critical. This includes looking for mentors, attending seminars and workshops, reading books, and actively participating in discussions with professionals in your field of interest.

Immersion in a learning culture broadens your horizons and increases your prospects of financial success. Ultimately, education and constant learning serve as the foundation for wealth growth. By investing in your knowledge and abilities, you give yourself the ability to make educated decisions, adapt to changing circumstances, and seize profitable opportunities.

Practical Tips for Leveraging Community to Build Wealth
Building money through community is not just a sound plan, but also a rewarding experience. Here are some practical strategies for utilizing the community to create wealth:

Network strategically: Surround yourself with others who have similar goals and desires. Attend business events, join professional groups, and participate in online communities to broaden your network. Engage in meaningful conversations, share ideas, and look for prospective partnerships or collaborations.

Seek mentorship: Look for experienced mentors in your community who can offer direction and share their wealth-building knowledge. Look for people who have attained the degree of accomplishment you desire and are willing to share their expertise. Their insights can help you avoid pitfalls, overcome obstacles, and expedite your wealth-building journey.

Collaborate on investments: Pooling resources with others in your community can help you expand your investing options. Consider creating investment clubs, real estate syndications, or crowdfunding campaigns. Sharing the financial burden and leveraging collective expertise allows you to access larger and more lucrative investment opportunities.

Share information and resources: Building wealth entails not just amassing goods, but also sharing knowledge and resources with others. Be willing to teach and learn from your community. Share insightful thoughts, propose beneficial tools or resources, and offer assistance to other members. The more you give to the community, the more you'll get in return.

Stay informed: Keep up with the latest trends, market insights, and investment possibilities in your community. Attend seminars, webinars, and workshops to keep learning and expanding your expertise. Staying educated allows you to make sound judgments and seize attractive wealth-building chances.

Remember that building wealth through community requires a team effort. You may speed your path to financial success by actively interacting with your community, building important connections, and using the collective power of information and resources.

To summarize, developing wealth through community is a powerful and successful method of achieving financial success. By surrounding yourself with like-minded people who are also striving for financial success, you can obtain vital insights, support, and chances that will help you get there faster.

Now is the time for you to take action that will help you reach your financial goals.

Embracing a Wealthy Mindset in All Areas of Life

So I resolved to adopt a new perspective on wealth—one that would allow me to take control of my finances and construct a system that would not just manage but also generate wealth while giving me freedom and choices.

This thinking is what I refer to as the "wealthy mindset."

It's astonishing to see people who appear to be doing well in their businesses or occupations but are never able to reach important goals because they lack the courage or mindset to do so.
They live in maintenance mode, unable to do more than the essentials and never feeling financially secure or optimistic about the future. They are in a rat race, have some resources, but are concerned about the future because they are unsure whether they have a clear method to sustain what they have accomplished.
These people are locked in sufficiency, never achieving abundance or actual affluence due to a fear of failure or not measuring up.
Are you one of them? Or do you sometimes fit into this category?

Many of these people could be affluent if they simply had a more adventurous mindset. If only they knew how to establish money streams without fear and determined to learn how to handle, create, and consolidate their wealth more effectively and boldly.
This Wealthy Mindset challenges you to overcome the fear that hinders you from pursuing mega-opportunity and focusing on prospects for advancement. It allows you to raise your standards even in the face of adversity, fear, or a demanding environment.

This thinking is a catalyst! A spark that produces amazing outcomes. Today, I encourage you to move beyond what you're accustomed to. I strongly advise you to embrace and master the abundant attitude.

Interestingly, developing this mindset is not a skill reserved for the wealthy or privileged few. It's a skill that everyone can learn and master, regardless of history or current financial circumstances.

CHAPTER 11

CONCLUSION

That single decision changed everything.
I got to where I am now because of that one choice.

I fear to think what would have happened if I hadn't made the decision to change that day.
Now, I'm not saying things have been easy since then; they haven't.
I Struggled because I was unfamiliar with the notions of momentum and sustainability.
My aspirations were unreasonable, unsustainable, and often counterproductive.
And then, when I didn't meet my goals, I'd beat myself up and slip into depression and sadness.
DOES THIS SOUND FAMILIAR?
You eventually stand up, just to fall back down because you bit off more than you could chew.
It happened to me more than I care to recall because I didn't set the correct goals.
I didn't have the correct goals because I didn't have the right priorities.
I didn't set the correct priorities since I wasn't serious.
I thought I was serious, but I didn't know what that meant.
Now I am as serious as a heart attack, and I will not accept anything less than complete triumph.

It's time to organize your priorities and establish concrete goals for success.
If you don't, it will be impossible to achieve your goals.
By not taking action, you are telling life that you are content with the way things are.
Success and failure are not unintended consequences.
YOU CHOOSE YOUR DESTINY.
You enjoy feeling fantastic and driven, but fail to follow through.
You don't take action because you lack an achievement mentality.
Instead, you pursue transitory joys.
I've been there, and I'm about to tell you something you already know.
Chasing pleasure will not bring you happiness; in fact, it will do the opposite.
That's because we aren't wired that way.

We are men, and we are meant to build and conquer.

The only time chasing pleasure will make you happy is after a long day at work, when it has been earned.

And, more crucially, if you are impoverished, you cannot afford to seek pleasure.
The future for pleasure-seeking guys is not promising.

You give up your shot at greatness for pizza, beer, and watching men exercise.
The price you pay for prioritizing pleasure is your happiness.
You spend the rest of your life bound to a desk beneath fluorescent lights, doing something you despise.

Crack the code of Becoming a lifetime millionaire

After three decades, you are fifty, pale, obese, bald, bent, and tired.
You exist to pay for a house, a car, a woman, and children that you are unable to afford.
This is the reality for MOST men.
AND THAT IS IF YOU'RE LUCKY.
If you're unlucky, you'll have to pay alimony and child support so you can see your children every other weekend.
I saw it with my own eyes.
Life isn't a trial run.

You only have one shot, and the world doesn't care if you succeed or fail.
If you're a young guy, I understand that this may be difficult to see right now, but you have to trust me.
The price you pay for all of your youth's mistakes, you pay with compound interest

I'm writing this book because I'm concerned that you don't completely comprehend what that means.
Every shot you miss at 20 will cost you exponentially more by the time you reach 30.
That $20,000 investment you did not make in yourself at 20 now costs you $200,000 at 30.

I'm concerned that you don't have the appropriate priorities.
If you are still living in your mother's basement, your first, second, and third priorities should be to move out.

Please understand that I do not wish for you to lead a monastic life.
I want you to have women.

I want you to feel confident as a gamer.
But I want you to have all of this after you've established the fundamentals, not before.
You're trying to have dessert before supper.
That harem of lovely women will not cover your rent.
You'll still have to shuffle into work on Monday morning to make someone else richer.
Having a harem is fun, but nothing beats doing work you enjoy and controlling your own time.
I've experienced both, and I can tell you from experience.
I don't want you to wind up like most guys: a broken husk of a man trudging through life.
I do not want you to accept mediocrity.
I want you to accept nothing less of greatness beginning today.
That implies it's time to set your priorities once and for all.

PRIORITIES
1) HEALTH.
Your health is now your first most important priority because you only have one body.
You will die if you do not have health.
That includes eating well, getting in shape, exercising daily, and getting enough sleep.

2) WEALTH.
Your number two priority right now is to make money.
That sounds materialistic, because it is. The slavery system you were born into is based on money.

People with no money have no options because everything in life is expensive.
Every situation you face can be fixed or considerably improved with money.
However, in order to generate real money and improve your life, you must become your own boss.
When you aren't your own boss, your fortune is determined by how much another man decides to give you.
To generate genuine money, you must start your own business.
Investing in your own business is the most valuable investment you can make.
When you own your own firm, you control a money-making machine.
Except for your business, everyone in your life wants what you have.
Your business is the only thing that provides.
As a result, you must prioritize your company's success.
You are now married to money.
Married to the Money.

3) LIFESTYLE
Your lifestyle will define your path in life.
If you're partying and getting up at noon, success will be impossible.
You need to be disciplined, dedicated, and determined.
That includes waking up early, getting organized, and managing your finances.

4) Relationships.
Personal relationships are now the least important aspect of your new life of kicking ass and taking names.
That's because a successful man is inherently busy.

Every social relationship has social obligations, and you only have seven nights per week.

Most of those nights will now be devoted to priority number one: creating money.

People are only one of the things that must be sacrificed on the altar of greatness.

There is an additional level of precedence in your interactions.

Family (If you have a close family).
Old friends/girlfriend
New Friends
Casual Dating.

As you can see, casual dating has become your very lowest priority.

If you actually want to advance, you should limit your interactions with women.

And deep down, they don't want to be your number one priority; in fact, they'll punish you for it.

Nothing appeals more to a woman than a man on a mission who keeps himself just out of reach.

GOALS

So, now that you've identified your priorities, it's time to make goals.
To set goals, use the S.M.A.R.T goal system, which stands for:

Specific : You have a definite goal and objective in mind.
Measurable – You may measure your progress toward achieving that goal.
Actionable – You are willing and capable of taking action to achieve your goal.

Relevant - Your goal is practical and addresses the main pain issue for one of your four priorities.
Timebound: Your goal has an end-of-year deadline.
This implies that each year, you will create four realistic goals based on your four life priorities.
Then you'll spend the entire year pursuing these objectives as if you had a gun to your head.

You will not think ten years from now since you cannot anticipate the future.
Instead, you're going to put your blinders on and ignore everything that gets in the way.

You're going to think, act, and speak like the CEO of Me, Inc., and live your life quarterly.
Every year, you will analyze your performance and make necessary adjustments.

Here's how to organize your four yearly goals in order of priority:
1) WEALTH.
You will live and die by this objective.
To achieve my wealth objective this year, I wrote two high-quality books. People told me it takes a year to write a good book, but I finished it in three months, working 15 hours every day.

Then I tried it again with my second book. That is how seriously I took achieving this goal.
As a result, I have decimated my wealth target.
A realistic aim for you would be to increase your income by $20,000.

2) HEALTH.

Your health objective is the second most important goal.

For the majority of you, presuming you're healthy, this will be a physical objective.

A realistic aim for a beginning trainee is to gain 20 pounds. of lean muscle to your frame.

3) LIFESTYLE

Your lifestyle objective is the third most significant goal.

My lifestyle goal this year was to relocate to Thailand.

It took a lot of preparation to get here, but it was the best decision I've made this year.

A reasonable aim for you is to become a minimalist by keeping all of your possessions under 200 items.

4) Relationships.

Your relationship aim is now the fourth and least significant one.

A realistic goal is to find a supportive girlfriend who will accept your quest.

Now that you've laid the groundwork, you can enjoy yourself.

Now that you've worked hard, gone to the gym, and been disciplined, you may start playing with girls.

There's nothing wrong with committing a few evenings to women when you've got things together.

Everything I'm about to tell you, you already know.

You understand that you need to make a change

You know you deserve more from life.

You've thought about it long enough.

You now have a roadmap.

Now you know what you need to do.

You now have no more excuses.

Now is the time to make it happen.

www.ingramcontent.com/pod-product-compliance
Lightning Source LLC
Chambersburg PA
CBHW052206220526
45471CB00004B/1836